D1558988

MARK'S TREATMENT
OF THE
JEWISH LEADERS

SUPPLEMENTS TO
NOVUM TESTAMENTUM

VOLUME LI

LEIDEN
E. J. BRILL
1978

MARK'S TREATMENT
OF THE
JEWISH LEADERS

BY

MICHAEL J. COOK

LEIDEN
E. J. BRILL
1978

ISBN 90 04 05785 4

Copyright 1978 by E. J. Brill, Leiden, The Netherlands

To Samuel Sandmel,
Teacher and Colleague

TABLE OF CONTENTS

Acknowledgements IX
List of Abbreviations XI

I. Introductory Overview 1
   The Subject of This Study 1
   The Nature of Our Approach 7
   The Problem of Mark's Provenance 10

II. Fundamental Methodological Considerations 15
    The Question of the Evangelists' Familiarity with the
      Jewish Leadership Groups They Present to Us . . 15
    The Implications of Matthew's and Luke's Dependence
      on Mark for Their Portrayal of Certain Jewish Leader-
      ship Groups 18
    The Degree of Mark's Dependence on His Sources for
      His Familiarity with Jewish Leadership Groups . . 28

III. Two Pre-Markan Controversy Collections 29
     Why Two Camps of Conspirators in Mark? 29
     M. Albertz' Theory of Two Pre-Markan Controversy
       Collections 31
     Assessing Albertz' Proposal 34
     Redefining the Scope of the Two Proposed Controversy
       Collections 43

IV. The Influence of a Pre-Markan Passion Tradition on Mark's
    Treatment of Jewish Leadership Groups 52
    Jewish Leadership Groups in the Pre-Markan Passion
      Tradition 52
    Mark's Redactional Procedures 58
    Assessing the Analysis by P. Winter 67
    Mark's Redactional Problems in Incorporating the Phar-
      isee/Herodian Source 73

V. Implications for the Historian 77
   Summary 77
   Implications of Our Study for the Historian 78
   Obstacles confronting the historian 78

The distinctiveness of the scribes and Pharisees in the
    Markan treatment   81
The interest of historians in the scribes and Pharisees .   83
Scribes and Pharisees in Mark: the significance of our
    proposals   85

Works Consulted   98
Index of Authors   103

ACKNOWLEDGEMENTS

I thank the Hebrew Union College-Jewish Institute of Religion for a generous grant subsidizing a portion of the cost of publishing this volume.

I also express my gratitude to Ms. Lori Puthoff for assistance in preparing the final draft, and to the library staff for help in securing the materials needed. The support of my wife, Ruth, and my children, David, Benjamin, and Maia, was unfailing and indispensable.

My deep appreciation also for the encouragement and criticisms by Samuel Sandmel and Ellis Rivkin, among others. Any errors in judgment or fact are, of course, my own.

MICHAEL J. COOK
Hebrew Union College-Jewish Institute of Religion
Cincinnati, Ohio
February 1978

LIST OF ABBREVIATIONS

BJRL	*Bulletin of the John Rylands Library.*
CBQ	*Catholic Biblical Quarterly.*
EB	*Encyclopaedia Biblica.* New York, 1899.
HTR	*Harvard Theological Review.*
HUCA	*Hebrew Union College Annual.*
IB	*Interpreter's Bible.* New York, 1951.
IDB	*Interpreter's Dictionary of the Bible.* New York, 1962.
IDB Suppl. Vol.	*Interpreter's Dictionary of the Bible*, Supplementary Volume. Nashville, 1976.
Interp.	*Interpretation.*
JBibRelig	*Journal of Bible and Religion.*
JBL	*Journal of Biblical Literature.*
JE	*The Jewish Encyclopedia.* New York, 1901.
JES	*Journal of Ecumenical Studies.*
JR	*Journal of Religion.*
JTS	*Journal of Theological Studies.*
NovT	*Novum Testamentum.*
NTS	*New Testament Studies.*
RHR	*Revue de l'histoire des religions.*
ZNW	*Zeitschrift für die neutestamentliche Wissenschaft.*
ZTK	*Zeitschrift für Theologie und Kirche.*

CHAPTER ONE

INTRODUCTORY OVERVIEW

The Subject of This Study

In the Synoptic tradition, Jesus frequently appears in conflict with various Jewish leadership elements, primarily "scribes," "Pharisees," and "chief priests," and, to a lesser degree, "elders," "Herodians," and "Sadducees." In the Fourth Gospel, these titles often yield to the more encompassing term, "the Jews."

These controversy traditions have long engaged scholarly interest for they have great bearing on significant dimensions of gospel study: they figure prominently in attempts to define the various modes of pre-70 Judaism and Jesus' distinctiveness from each of them; they are the central focus in efforts to trace the escalation of hostility between Jesus and his political opponents which culminated in his arrest and condemnation; and often they convey essentials of Jesus' ethics and theological outlook.

Despite the immense scholarship on these passages, certain fundamental methodological considerations in analyzing them have generally gone overlooked. Until these considerations are brought to bear, new analyses of the controversy traditions will merely reproduce errors of the past.

The Synoptic Gospels, as is commonly recognized, do not furnish us with clear definitions of the Jewish leadership groups presumed to have been active in Jesus' time. It is naturally supposed that the Evangelists felt no need to clarify what they assumed was already self-evident to their listeners or readers. We will contend, however, that the Evangelists *themselves* were unclear as to who all these Jewish leadership groups had actually been in Jesus' time; they did not adequately define and describe them or adequately distinguish among them because they *could* not. Moreover, some of the group titles ("chief priests," "Herodians," "elders") are merely general constructs, i.e., literary devices serving the convenience of the Synoptists themselves and lifted from their sources; they are not reflective of leadership groups actually functioning in Jesus' time or later.

Most of these titles—Pharisees, scribes, chief priests, elders, Herodians, Sadducees—appear not only in Mark but in the later Synoptics as well. Regrettably, this circumstance has bolstered confidence in the reliability of the gospels' portrayal of these leadership elements, inducing some scholars to refer indiscriminately to any or all the Synoptics plus Acts in defining a given group. We will contend, however, that treatments of Jewish leadership groups in Matthew and Luke are essentially but preservation and occasionally free embellishment of the Markan account, [1] and that the appearance of a given leadership element in the later Synoptics does not necessarily enhance our knowledge of that group or even confirm Mark's assumption that such a group confronted Jesus during his ministry.

Some of the Palestinian leadership groups presumed active in Jesus' day (e.g., "scribes," "chief priests," "Sadducees") were not prominent after 70 C.E. The later Evangelists, further chronologically removed from these authorities than was Mark, could have had no recent first-hand acquaintance with them. Moreover, most or all of the Synoptists were also geographically removed from these groups. Aside from testimony of Christian tradition, we have no assurance that any of the Synoptists had personal acquaintance with the Palestinian scene; nor is there reason to presume that any of the Jewish leadership groups, aside from the Pharisees, frequented regions of the Diaspora. From what sources, then, do the Evangelists derive their knowledge of pre-70 Palestinian-based Jewish authorities? Clearly, for Matthew and Luke, Mark constitutes one such source; indeed, it is possible that, on the subject of the authority groups, Mark is their only source. There is no way of demonstrating that any of their sources other than Mark mentioned·Jewish leadership groups *by title*; in fact, peculiarities in the Matthaean and Lukan portrayals of these authorities imply that the later Synoptists take their cue solely from Mark, with Luke most likely dependent on Matthew as well. Any fuller treatments of these groups by Matthew and Luke can more plausibly be ascribed to the

---

[1] We thus uphold the generally accepted theory of Markan priority. William R. Farmer has attacked this solution in *The Synoptic Problem: A Critical Analysis*, New York, 1964. See, in response, the reviews by Frederick C. Grant, *Interp.* 19 (1965), 352-354, and F. W. Beare, *JBL* 84 (1965), 295-297, and the lengthy analysis by C. H. Talbert and E. V. McKnight, "Can the Griesbach Hypothesis Be Falsified?" *JBL* 91 (1972), 338-368. See also T. A. Burkill, *New Light on the Earliest Gospel: Seven Markan Studies*, Ithaca, 1972, 74 n. 6; Joseph B. Tyson, *A Study of Early Christianity*, New York, 1973, 183-190; N. Perrin, *Rediscovering the Teaching of Jesus*, New York, 1967, 35.

authors' improvisation than to dependence on other presumed source material. 2

Precisely because Matthew and Luke lack personal familiarity with most of these groups, they often obscure rather than clarify the Markan information. Scholars who practice indiscriminate recourse to all the Synoptists, and even to John, 3 in fashioning "composite" portraits of

---

2 At this juncture, we indicate our belief that Luke depended on Matthew as well as Mark. While this matter is somewhat peripheral to our major concerns, it does surface occasionally. The analysis penned several decades ago by M. S. Enslin merits citation at length: "...I find myself more and more skeptical not about the age of Q but of its very existence, and am inclined to feel that it is an unnecessary and unwarranted assumption serving to account for material common to Matthew and Luke which can be more satisfactorily explained on the hypothesis that one of them used the other. And it appears to me highly probable that Luke was the one who did the borrowing.... After removing the 'triple tradition' from Matthew and Luke as coming from Mark and the 'double tradition' as due to Luke's use of Matthew, ... there remains a considerable residue in Matthew and Luke. While parts of this material can be safely classed as legendary, in some cases probably haggadic expansions of the earlier narrative made by the evangelists themselves, that accounts for but a part of the special material. There seems no good reason to doubt that both Matthew and Luke had special sources of information from which they drew. The nature of these sources, however, is by no means clear.... [The] M source has not secured many champions, and has little to commend it, but several competent scholars are agreed that Luke did make use of a connected source which at times, as in the Passion narrative, he preferred to Mark. But, after all, the whole matter of L depends on the question as to the extent to which Lucan differences can be explained as the work of Luke himself. It appears to me that the sole value of L is that it gives relief to puzzled interpreters of Luke who cannot bring themselves to allow Luke to make (or make up) history, but find it necessary to postulate another source for him to draw upon.... It would appear to me probable that in the coming years both Matthew and Luke will be obliged to accept responsibility for forsaking Mark when they each thought they could pen better stories. Furthermore, just as considerable material which was formerly marked 'Matthew special' or 'Luke special' may not unreasonably be considered the evangelists' own revamping or rewriting of Markan matter, so I am inclined to feel a fresh study of the special material of Luke in the light of its being a possible adaption of Matthew would not be wasted.... All Christian tradition was not restricted to sources as we so easily imagine..." (*Christian Beginnings*, repr., New York, 1956, 433-435). See also A. M. Farrer, "On Dispensing with Q," in D. E. Nineham, ed., *Studies in the Gospels: Essays in Memory of R. H. Lightfoot*, Oxford, 1955, 55-86; S. Petrie, " 'Q' Is Only What You Make It," *NovT* 3 (1959), 28-33.

3 We do not treat the Gospel According to John in this volume. As a source for Jesus' relations with Jewish leadership groups, John is even further removed from the earliest traditions than is Matthew or Luke: "Taking the data of the Fourth Gospel in relation to the earlier formulations, it would seem that its references may be understood as the use of tradition of rather long standing, but without any high degree of verisimilitude. The obvious line of distinction for the religious groups was between the Christians as such and 'the Jews,' but, since there were identifications in the earlier sources, the Gospel writer varied his usual reference to 'the Jews' by citing, upon occasion, particular groups.... The identifications of the Fourth Gospel are not

each leadership element are, therefore, being highly injudicious in their use of sources. Any study on this subject must necessarily focus primarily on Mark, as we shall presently do in this volume.

We seek to answer the following questions: How familiar is the author of Mark with the various Jewish leadership groups he presents to us? What are his sources of knowledge, and how does he use them? Is the Markan portrayal of Jewish authorities and their confrontations with Jesus historically reliable?

We will contend that the author himself knows very little about the Jewish leadership groups he presumes were active in Jesus' time; that he depends very heavily on three written sources which he incorporates into his gospel and with great resourcefulness accommodates to one another; and that the resulting portrayal of Jewish authorities—while reflecting considerable redactional skill—is nevertheless artificial, and not a reliable index for the historian of Jesus' ministry, especially because Mark's sources and his editorial treatment of them reflect concerns of a context far later than Jesus' ministry itself. Precisely because the Markan material on Jewish leaders is so largely determinative of the treatments of these groups by Matthew and Luke, our conclusions concerning Mark carry sobering ramifications for the controversy traditions in the Synoptics as a whole, not to mention the many scholarly studies relying upon them.

Many scholars have expressed certainty that written sources underlie clusters of controversy pericopae in Mark—especially 2:1-3:6 and parts of Chapters 11-12. We will draw upon but redirect their work by indicating *the* tell-tale clue as to the actual parameters of Mark's sources: his radical segregation of the Jewish leadership groups into two separate camps of conspirators—chief priests + scribes + elders, on the one hand, and Pharisees + Herodians, on the other. This pattern of rigid compartmentalization and the occasional departures therefrom can best (and perhaps can only) be explained on the assumption that Mark utilizes: 1) an early Passion source, furnishing him with chief priests, scribes and elders, based in Jerusalem; 2) a source focusing on scribes only, setting them in Jerusalem; and 3) a

---

made with vital connection of fact. To the Gospel's public, as to its writer, it did not greatly matter, since 'the Jews' were the party of the opposition, whether particular groups of Jews were correctly designated, so long as the narrative itself was convincing" (D. W. Riddle, *Jesus and the Pharisees*, Chicago, 1928, 158; see, more generally, 44-52, 145-166). On John's use of "the Jews," see the pertinent sections of T. L. Schram, *The Use of Ioudaios in the Fourth Gospel*, Utrecht, 1974, and his bibliographical listings.

source focusing on Pharisees and Herodians, possibly set in a Galilean context.

Because the first two sources mentioned "scribes" but never "Pharisees," while the third mentioned "Pharisees" but never "scribes," Mark construes scribes and Pharisees to have been distinct from one another. The two terms refer to the same element of society, but Mark, unfamiliar with who "scribes" had been, fails to detect the synonymity of the usage, and therefore presents us with two groups rather than one. The modern problem of differentiating between scribes and Pharisees in the gospels thus originates with Mark's sources and with his attempts to accommodate them to one another. Because this root of the problem has not been recognized, most New Testament scholars perpetuate Mark's own misconception, and pursue the unavailing task of distinguishing scribes from Pharisees, usually relying on Mk. 2:16 and 7:1,5 in conjunction with Acts 23:9, and advancing the notion that scribes are a subgroup of Pharisees or their intellectual elite. The appearance of "scribes" in 2:16 and 7:1,5 is, however, redactional, inserted by Mark in the interest of a literary accommodation of his three sources to one another; and these Markan interpolations have influenced Acts at 23:9.

As a matter of fact, in many controversy pericopae, the very appearance of Jewish authority groups is artificial; in these passages, the group names have simply been plugged into earlier traditions not initially mentioning them. The controversies therein described may reflect not confrontations between Jewish authorities and Jesus but retrojections of tensions between Jewish teachers and the later church, with the responses attributed to Jesus intended as paradigms for the responses of his later "disciples" in disputation with Jewish opponents of *their* day. We are not denying that Jesus himself engaged in controversies with religious opponents (particularly the Pharisees), but we do deny that the gospels can be confidently used to confirm the occurrence of specific disputations or to reconstruct their exact substance or even, in some cases, to identify the disputants.

It is wise, in this regard, to be cognizant of the context of the Evangelists: all the Synoptic Gospels were completed against a backdrop of insecurity for the early Christian communities. Aside from the problems internal to the communities, there were external threats, among them Roman persecution and also harassment from the Pharisees/rabbis. The Synoptic Gospels represent, in part, reactions to both these external threats; the controversy traditions are a function of this late response.

The Gospel According to Mark is here again most significant because it is the earliest such response we have, and because it sets the patterns for the others. It was composed during the very years of the great Jewish revolt in Palestine, 66-73, [4] a rebellion fraught with potentially serious consequences for Christians in the Empire at large. Only recently, the Christian community in Rome, designated scapegoat by Nero for the fire of 64, had experienced its first taste of Roman persecution. [5] The Jewish revolt in Palestine now offered a further chilling prospect: that Roman disaffection with the Jews, and the Roman vengeance inevitably to follow, might spill over and redound to the further disadvantage of the Christian community.

For in the eyes of many a heathen, Christians seemed hardly distinguishable from Jews: Jesus and his initial followers were all reputed to have been Jews; Christian missionaries cited Jewish Scriptures, accepted fundamentals of Jewish theology, addressed audiences in Jewish synagogues, and drew new members from the ranks of Gentiles many of whom had originally been attracted by Jewish proselytism. Moreover, earlier, in 49, the expulsion of Jews from Rome entailed the expulsion of Christians along with them. [6] It was, accordingly, in the Christian interest now, around 70, to distinguish the image of Christian from that of Jew, and to persuade Rome that she and Christianity were natural allies, sharing as they did a common enemy, the Jews.

---

[4] J. Moffatt, *An Introduction to the Literature of the New Testament*, New York, 1923, 211ff., presents in convenient tabular form the spectrum of earlier scholarly opinion as to the dates of the Synoptic Gospels, with over fifty opinions on Mark alone (ranging from 44 to 130+ C.E., more than half between 64 and 73). Later scholarship can be readily gathered from Enslin, *op. cit.*, 385ff.; P. Feine, J. Behm, and W. G. Kümmel, *Introduction to the New Testament*, trans. A. J. Mattill, Jr., Nashville, 1965, 70ff.; R. P. Martin, *Mark: Evangelist and Theologian*, Trowbridge, 1972, Chapter 3. A variety of important positions are represented in the following studies: C. C. Torrey, "The Date of Mark," *Documents of the Primitive Church*, New York, 1941, 1-40; A. Harnack, *The Date of the Acts and of the Synoptic Gospels*, London, 1911, 126-133; B. H. Streeter, *The Four Gospels*, London, 1924, 488ff.; B. W. Bacon, *The Gospel of Mark: Its Composition and Date*, New Haven, 1925, especially Chapters 1-4, 20-24; B. H. Branscomb, *The Gospel of Mark*, London, 1937, xxix ff.; S. G. F. Brandon, "The Date of the Markan Gospel," *NTS* 7 (1960-1961), 126ff.; R. A. Spivey and D. M. Smith, Jr., *Anatomy of the New Testament*, 2d ed., New York, 1974, 83-84. We are personally disposed toward the early 70's. See Enslin (as above); T. A. Burkill, *op. cit.*, 264; Brandon, *Jesus and the Zealots*, Manchester, 1967, Chapter 5; J. R. Donahue, *Are You the Christ? The Trial Narrative in the Gospel of Mark*, Missoula, Montana, 1973, 131-132.

[5] Tacitus, *Annals* XV. 44.

[6] Suetonius, *Life of Claudius* 25; Acts 18:2.

It is here that the traditions of controversy between Jesus and Jewish leadership groups well-served the Markan interest. They demonstrated to Rome that, from the Christians' perspective, it was the Jewish leaders rather than Rome who were responsible for Jesus' condemnation, and that they had been involved in plotting his destruction well in advance of Pilate's first encounter with Jesus in Jerusalem. [7] Rome, therefore, should realize that Christians bore her no ill will for the death of their Lord (despite the Roman means of execution), and that Christians should not be suspected of the kind of subversive activity now shown to be characteristic of the Jewish enemy. The founder of Christianity was a man of peace, loyal to Rome, [8] who had himself perceived, well in advance, that the Temple in Jerusalem would fall. [9] He and his followers had been betrayed and rejected by the Jews, now the common enemy of Rome and Christianity alike.

The three sources from which Mark received his knowledge of Jesus' enemies probably antedated the Jewish revolt. They served their own function in their earlier day, distinct in some respects from the use to which Mark himself later applied them. They helped Gentile-Christians rationalize why a movement which had begun within the confines of Judaism had later emerged as predominantly Gentile in make-up: Jesus had turned to the Gentiles because the Jewish leaders had refused to accept the Good News and instead had harassed Jesus and his disciples for alleged political trespass and for departure from Jewish ritual and calendrical observance and for messianic pretensions presumptuous and devoid of substance. The persistence of this harassment contributed to the creation of the controversy collections, later revised and incorporated and accommodated to one another by Mark.

The Nature of Our Approach

Redaction criticism, "the analysis of the editorial work of the writers in relation to their sources," [10] has become a dominant mode of current gospel scholarship. It involves "two major operations: literary analysis to uncover what an author does with his material, and an act of judgment on why he does what he does, or, in other words, on his religious and theological intent." [11] No longer are the Evangelists to be viewed

---

[7] An overt statement of their conspiracy appears as early as Mk. 3:6; Pilate does not meet Jesus until 15:1.

[8] Mk. 12:13ff.

[9] Mk. 13:1ff.

[10] Spivey and Smith, *op. cit.*, 81.

[11] Donahue, *op. cit.*, 2.

simply as collectors and arrangers of traditions [12] but as those who
decide what to preserve and how to present it, and who superimpose
their own perspectives on the traditional material, each Evangelist
applying the tradition "in creative, constructive and different ways,"
each seeking "to speak with relevance and power to his own situation." [13] And especially in the case of Mark are these concerns
important, for

> Mark's situation differs from Matthew's and Luke's. From the outset,
> Matthew and Luke had access to a presentation which somehow was
> already formed. It consisted of an enlarged sketch which formed a
> unity created by one individual. In addition, Matthew and Luke used
> anonymous tradition.... Mark, on the other hand, has at his disposal
> only anonymous individual traditions, except for certain complexes
> and a passion narrative. Mark's achievement in shaping the tradition
> is thus incomparably greater. As far as we can tell, Mark is the first
> to bring the individualistic element to the forming and shaping of the
> tradition. [14]

Thus, redaction criticism clearly supplements and redirects in a
valuable way the insights of source and form criticism. In particular,
it has served to concentrate attention on the ways in which Mark's
theological concerns are reflected through his editorial policies such

---

[12] The perspective of M. Dibelius, earlier this century, presents a striking contrast
with that of redaction criticism: "The literary understanding of the synoptics begins
with the recognition that they are collections of material. The composers are only
to the smallest extent authors. They are principally collectors, vehicles of tradition,
editors. Before all else their labour consists in handing down, grouping, and working
over the material which has come to them.... It can be estimated *in how lowly a degree*
after all St. Mark and St. Matthew may pass as *authors*. These matters are no longer
in doubt..." (*From Tradition to Gospel*, trans. B. L. Woolf, New York, 1935, 3;
italics ours).

[13] Spivey and Smith, *op. cit.*, 81.

[14] W. Marxsen, *Mark the Evangelist: Studies on the Redaction History of the
Gospel*, trans. J. Boyce *et al*, Nashville, 1969, 19. See also G. Bornkamm: "The
Synoptic writers show—all three and each in his own special way—by their editing
and construction, by their selection, inclusion and omission, and not least by what at
first sight appears an insignificant, but on closer examination is seen to be characteristic treatment of the traditional material, that they are by no means mere collectors
and handers-on of the tradition, but also interpreters of it" (G. Bornkamm, G. Barth
and H. J. Held, *Tradition and Interpretation in Matthew*, trans. P. Scott, Philadelphia,
1963, 11). A delineation of the differences between redaction criticism and form
criticism may be found in R. H. Stein, "What Is Redactionsgeschichte?" *JBL* 88
(1969), 45-56; see also Martin, *op. cit.*, 47ff.; Perrin, *op. cit.*, opening chapter, and
What Is Redaction Criticism?, Philadelphia, 1969; cf. also J. Rohde, *Rediscovering
the Teaching of the Evangelists*, trans. D. Barton, Philadelphia, 1969; Donahue, *op.
cit.*, 5ff., 35-48. For surveys of redaction-critical work on Mark, see listings by
Donahue, 5 n. 1.

that one is tempted to study even limited aspects of Mark's Gospel not piecemeal but rather in relationship to Mark's overall patterns of editorial creativity and in the light of the theological stance of his Gospel as a whole.

This present volume also happens to focus on a limited dimension of Mark's Gospel—his treatment of Jewish leadership groups—but we do not feel it appropriate to proceed entirely along redaction critical lines; we are, however, sensitive to these concerns. The title of our work does indicate our recognition of Mark's own role in determining the image of Jewish leadership groups in his Gospel. Time and again, moreover, we shall stress the editorial skill with which Mark himself uses his sources and, through extensive improvisation, accommodates them to one another in the light of his personal concerns, for Mark is definitely an author, not merely one who pastes together unaltered scraps. Above all, we recognize that Mark, not to mention the later Evangelists, has produced what is primarily a work of theology far more concerned to elicit faith in Jesus as the Christ than to convey accurate information about the historical Jesus and his social, political and geographical context, and that Mark has assigned the Jewish authorities a special function in terms of the theology of his drama.

Yet we are persuaded that, on the subject of the Jewish leadership groups, a preoccupation with redaction criticism can swing the pendulum too far, eclipsing rather than illuminating the very genuine contributions of source and form criticism. Earlier this century, a number of source and form critical studies did indeed focus on traditions of controversy between Jesus and Jewish authorities, and many of their conclusions elicited wide approval, and continue to do so. We feel, however, that because of questionable procedures these earlier studies now require reassessment. Since the preliminary spade work has yet to be satisfactorily accomplished, to approach this subject primarily from a redaction critical perspective is inappropriate; conclusions of earlier studies must first be readjusted. Only after we clarify the nature of Mark's sources on the Jewish leaders can we approach the problem of his redactional procedures in incorporating and embellishing this material. And even then we should acknowledge the subjective dimension of many redaction critical studies as is evidenced by the wide spectrum of scholarly conclusions concerning Mark's special motives and editorial practices. [15]

---

[15] See, e.g., H. C. Kee, *Community of the New Age: Studies in Mark's Gospel*, Philadelphia, 1977, 9 and nn. 48-49; Donahue, *op. cit.*, 210f.

It will thus become apparent that, despite the trend in New Testament scholarship to present Mark more as theological drama than as historical report, the questions we shall raise are more historical than theological. For the very nature of our investigation is to determine how familiar Mark himself was with the Jewish leadership groups, where he received his information about them, and how he used it in constructing the framework of his narrative line. We shall allude to the function he assigned the Jewish leaders in his theological drama, but this is hardly our central concern. Clearly, Mark was not what we would call an historian, but he needed a certain fundamental historical nucleus as a vehicle for his theological message, and the Jewish leadership groups formed part of this nucleus. To attain verisimilitude in presenting the Jewish authorities, Mark had to come into possession of at least minimal historical data. Regardless of the importance of Mark's editorializing, the historian is justified in attempting to determine whence arose the information Mark presents, and also in attempting to reconstruct the nature of these early traditions before they came, in whatever altered form, to assume their current place in the gospel literature.

Realistically speaking, source, form and redaction criticism should not be conceived of atomistically or independently of one another. At times, however, it will indeed appear that we are focusing on one or another approach in isolation from the others, but this is in the interests of clarity. The three approaches should nevertheless always be envisioned as impinging upon each other.

The Problem of Mark's Provenance

We believe that the Gospel According to Mark was composed in the Dispersion. Since this consideration is presupposed throughout this volume, it is appropriate to indicate the bases of our judgment.

Even while we affirm that Palestinian material underlies much of the content of Mark, we believe that the Gospel itself emanates from a Gentile-Christian environment outside Palestine. The precise provenance is not of critical concern, though we consider the best candidate to be Rome itself.

The best study of the problem, still not outdated, is B. W. Bacon's *Is Mark a Roman Gospel?* [16] Since this book is no longer easily acces-

---

[16] Cambridge, Mass., 1919.

sible, we present its fundamental arguments in condensed form: The tradition of a Roman provenance of Mark has persisted "in spite of a strong tendency ... to carry back the origin of the Gospels to a period antecedent to the dispersion of the Twelve from Palestine" (p. 7). The tradition that Mark (not himself a disciple) wrote in Rome some time after Peter had died there is thus not at all "in the interest of apologetic; it was rather found inconvenient" (p. 11). Hence, the tradition very possibly has a historical basis: "The place where ... a given anonymous writing began to circulate is matter of public knowledge. The allegations of tradition [on this point] ... are relatively trustworthy, especially if free from (and still more if opposed to) apologetic interest" (p. 10).

Second, while the Papian testimony concerning Mark is not reliable in all particulars, and while it may rest to some extent on the pseudonymous I Peter (ca. 87), its identification of Mark with Rome may be correct. I Peter was probably itself a Roman writing showing (in 5:13) "the special respect in which Mark was then held at Rome" in particular (p. 30). Papias would not have been "apt to take up the idea that Mark was a Roman Gospel, or having taken it up ... persistently to maintain and transmit it, if such were not the fact" (p. 31).

Third, "a document [such as Mark] which on its face makes so little pretense of authority could hardly be expected to attain such [extremely high] standing if emanating from some obscure region undistinguished as the seat of any 'apostolic' church" (p. 34). The "truly extraordinary" respect shown for it by Matthew and Luke "is difficult to account for unless the Gospel had already attained wide currency and acceptance, implying that it was vouched for in high quarters" (p. 34). "Once the larger Gospel of Matthew with its higher claims of apostolic authority had come into general use" (p. 37), the Gospel According to Mark should have faded into oblivion. A combination of its merits and its association with Peter would alone have been insufficient to maintain its high influence; we can better explain its continued importance as due to "the authority, position and influence of the community which first gave it currency" (p. 38). Antioch and Ephesus have, respectively, their own Gospels, and "tradition is absolutely silent as to [Markan] provenance from these regions" (p. 43). A Palestinian provenance for Mark is unlikely; "no gospel having such small pretensions to apostolicity could have won in Palestine the place which Mark came to occupy" (pp. 42-43).

Fourth, with regard to linguistic considerations, Mark uses and is influenced by the Septuagint, not the Hebrew Scriptures. That basic Christian traditions in Mark seem to have been translations from Aramaic carries no weight against Dispersion or Roman provenance; it is possible that Mark "consists largely, perhaps almost exclusively, of Aramaic documentary material, preserved in the archives of the church in Rome; for such material must have been carried everywhere from Palestine by primitive evangelists" (p. 49). Only if the actual editorial framework of Mark had been current in Aramaic could the Dispersion provenance of Mark be disproved (p. 53). While not conclusive in its own right, Mark's use of Latinisms (and to a greater extent than the other Evangelists) is certainly compatible with a theory of Roman provenance, [17] especially when in two instances (12:42 and 15:16) Greek is explained by Latin (pp. 53-54).

Fifth, added to these considerations are Mark's editorial glosses and explanations. The fact that "Mark seems to consider an accompanying translation necessary for his readers' benefit in all cases save the most commonplace" (p. 55) implies composition in the Dispersion. Mark's translation of Aramaic in no way implies his mastery of the language "as we must presuppose in a native or long resident of Jerusalem"; indeed, his treatment of 15:34-36 only attests to his unfamiliarity with this language (pp. 56-57).

Sixth, Mark is evidently considerably removed from and unfamiliar with local Palestinian geography and history (pp. 59ff.). [18]

Many other scholars have supported the theory of Roman provenance; others cite Egypt or Antioch. [19] We strongly dispute, however, views

[17] See listing in Feine, Behm and Kümmel, op. cit., 70; and Martin, op. cit., 64.

[18] See also P. J. Achtemeier, Mark, Philadelphia, Fortress, 1975, 115f.; cf. K. Niederwimmer, "Johannes Markus und die Frage nach dem Verfasser des zweiten Evangeliums," ZNW 58 (1967), 172-188.

[19] See Riddle, op. cit., and Brandon, Zealots, for whom Rome itself figures prominently in discussions of Mark; cf. also Martin, op. cit., 62; W. L. Lane, The Gospel of Mark, Grand Rapids, 1975, 24f.; V. Taylor, The Gospel According to St. Mark, 2d ed., New York, 1966, 32; Tyson, op. cit., 197; R. Pesch, Das Markusevangelium, I, Freiburg, 1976, 2. For an Egyptian provenance for Mark, see S. E. Johnson, A Commentary on the Gospel according to Mark, New York, 1960, 15; H. B. Swete, The Gospel according to St. Mark, London, 1927, xviii ff.; T. W. Manson, Studies in the Gospels, Manchester, 1962, 38ff.; J. Finegan, Mark of the Taw, Richmond, 1972 (fictionalized embellishment of this theory). For provenance in Antioch, see discussion in J. V. Bartlet, St. Mark, Edinburgh, 1922, 36f.; W. C. Allen, The Gospel according to St. Mark, London, 1915. A base in rural and small-town southern Syria is proposed by Kee, op. cit., 100-105, 176.

espousing a Palestinian provenance. [20] Some of these proceed along the following lines:

The expectation in Mark is that Jesus' resurrection appearances (or, according to another view, the impending Parousia) will occur in Galilee. A consideration of the tension between this Galilean setting, in Mark and Matthew, and the Jerusalem setting, in Luke, can lead one to infer that Mark cherished a personal interest in Galilee and that the Gospel could thus have indeed been written in Palestine rather than in the Graeco-Roman Dispersion. We feel, however, that the extensive and complicated discussion on the subject of the Galilean vs. the Jerusalem setting of the post-resurrection period has no ultimate bearing on the problem of where Mark himself wrote.

Mark's emphasis on Galilee may simply reflect the historical reality that Galilee was the native region of Jesus and of most of his disciples. Accordingly, when Mark alleges that the disciples fled from the Garden of Gethsemane, it is hardly surprising or significant that they would be portrayed as fleeing to Galilee; and when Jesus would appear following his resurrection, naturally he would appear where his followers were rather than where they were not. Matthew's actual recounting of a post-resurrection appearance in Galilee is a natural complement of Mark's narrative. The Galilean appearances reveal nothing substantive about the provenance of the Second Gospel. [21]

Even supposing that Mark had a theological motive for locating

---

[20] Presentation and discussion of these views are found in E. Lohmeyer, *Galiläa und Jerusalem*, Göttingen, 1936 and *Das Evangelium des Markus*, Göttingen, 1937; R. H. Lightfoot, *Locality and Doctrine in the Gospels*, London, 1938; cf. Kee, *op. cit.*, 7-8, 62, 102f.; N. Q. Hamilton, "Resurrection Tradition and the Composition of Mark," *JBL* 84 (1965), 415-421; Marxsen, *op. cit.*, Study Two; M. Karnetski, "Die galiläische Redaktion im Markusevangelium," *ZNW* 52 (1961), 228-272. See additional references in T. J. Weeden, *Mark—Traditions in Conflict*, Philadelphia, 1972, 111 n. 13. Note the more recent work by W. H. Kelber, *The Kingdom in Mark: a New Place and a New Time*, Philadelphia, 1974.

[21] It is Luke's location of the resurrection appearances in the vicinity of Jerusalem which is tendentious, not Mark's presumed anticipation of their occurrence in Galilee. Luke desires to demonstrate Christianity's birth from the mainstream of Judaism (Jerusalem) rather than from the fringes (Galilee), a concern manifested throughout Luke-Acts, especially in the portrayal of Jesus as faithful to the heart of Judaism and in the depiction of Paul as a loyal rabbinic Jew reared in Jerusalem at the feet of Gamaliel. See S. Sandmel, *A Jewish Understanding of the New Testament*, New York, 1960, 170ff., 185ff., 190ff., 254ff.; and *The Genius of Paul*, New York, 1970, 120ff.; Enslin, "Paul and Gamaliel," *JR* 7 (1927), 360-375; and "Once Again, Luke and Paul," *ZNW* 61 (1970), 253-271; J. Knox, *Chapters in a Life of Paul*, Nashville, 1950, 13-88; A. C. Purdy, "Paul the Apostle," *IDB*, III, 683-684; cf. also H. Conzelmann, *A History of Primitive Christianity*, trans. J. E. Steely, Nashville, 1973, 78-95.

Jesus' future appearance in Galilee, it would have arisen from Galilee's ethnic situation in the first century and the Septuagint's repeated association of Galilee with the Gentiles, both of these factors known to Mark. [22] Does the Galilean material require that Mark himself resided in the Holy Land? If a Galilean Christian community (of which Acts makes no mention, or even studiously avoids mention) existed and preserved traditions of Jesus in Galilee after the Crucifixion, this does not require Mark to have been either a Palestinian or personally familiar with Palestine, but only to have had access to these traditions when they were disseminated in the Dispersion. [23]

---

[22] See especially G. H. Boobyer, "Galilee and Galileans in St. Mark's Gospel," *BJRL* 35 (1952-1953), 334-348; cf. Karnetski, *art. cit.*, 238ff.; J. Schreiber, "Die Christologie des Markus," *ZTK* 58 (1961), 154-183.

[23] To be sure, it is not even certain whether Mark himself anticipated the resurrection appearances or the Parousia in Galilee. Only two verses are involved: 14:28 and 16:7; these are usually seen as glosses, presumably by Mark himself. We agree they are glosses; we deny they stem from Mark. We feel 14:28 is interpolated into material which Mark himself composed and hence is post-Markan. Moreover, Mark is himself responsible for anti-Petrine material (e.g., 8:32-34; 14:29-31, 66-72); 16:7 is pro-Petrine and was added by a later hand to neutralize Mark's bias. It is possible that 8:29-30 was similarly added. If 14:28 and 16:7 were interpolated by a later hand than Mark, they reflect nothing about Mark himself let alone about the Gospel's provenance. The reason for these interpolations is tied to the absence in Mark of any account of Jesus' post-resurrection appearances. Mk. 16:9-20 is clearly a late addition (see especially F. J. A. Hort and B. F. Westcott, *The New Testament in the Original Greek*, Cambridge and London, 1882, 28-51; Swete, *The Gospel according to St. Mark*, 3d ed., repr., London, 1920, ciii-cxiii), details of which are apparently gleaned from traditions found in Luke and John to round out the Markan account. Mk. 14:28 and 16:7 represent an earlier effort to render the Markan narrative more satisfying by indicating something of the nature of future developments after Jesus' death. 16:7 must be pre-Lukan because Luke rewrites it so as to allow a substitution of Jerusalem environs for Galilee. On the possibility that 14:28 and 16:7 are post-Markan, see F. C. Grant, "The Gospel According to St. Mark: Introduction and Exegesis," *IB*, VII, 879, 914-915.

CHAPTER TWO

FUNDAMENTAL METHODOLOGICAL CONSIDERATIONS

*The Question of the Evangelists' Familiarity with the Jewish
Leadership Groups They Present to Us*

When scholars treat gospel passages portraying scribes, Pharisees, Herodians, chief priests, and so on, naturally they are tempted to clarify precisely who these groups were in Jesus' day—who comprised them, what viewpoints they espoused, whose interests they represented. Presumably, this is a necessary procedure, but should it be our primary consideration? Our fundamental quest is not merely to determine for ourselves who these groups were in Jesus' time but also who the *Evangelists* presumed these groups were.

Scholars bent on discovering for themselves the identity of these Jewish leadership groups must supplement the meager data of the gospels. They search out mentions of Pharisees, Sadducees, etc., in Josephus and rabbinic literature, presuming that, by applying the latter data to those supplied by the gospels, they can secure a fuller understanding of gospel controversy traditions. Given this preoccupation, it is no wonder that the question of whether or not the Evangelists could adequately identify these groups is easily by-passed as beside the point.

And yet, this *is* the point! If our concern is not merely with the leadership groups themselves as much as with their exchanges with Jesus, then let us realize that the Evangelists are our only sources describing these groups in conjunction with Jesus. Josephus describes the Pharisees, Sadducees and the priesthood, as well as some messianic aspirants, but rarely mentions Jesus [1] and certainly conveys nothing

---

[1] Jesus' name appears once as an aid in identifying his relative James, in which case Josephus is focusing on James, not Jesus *(Antiquities* XX.ix.1 [xx.200]). On another occasion, Josephus mentions Jesus in a paragraph ostensibly affirming Josephus' acceptance of Jesus as the Christ *(Antiq.* XVIII.iii.3 [xviii.63-64]). For selected literature on the *Testimonium Flavianum,* see the Loeb edition of Josephus, trans. by Louis H. Feldman, IX, Cambridge, Mass., 1965, Appendix K, pp. 573-575; and the excursus prepared by P. Winter and included in the recent Vermes-Millar edition of E. Schürer's *The History of the Jewish People in the Age of Jesus Christ (175 B.C.-A.D. 135),* Vol. I, Edinburgh, 1973, 428-441. See also Sh. Pines, *An Arabic Version of the Testimonium Flavianum and Its Implications,* Jerusalem, 1971. Scholars skeptical

of any exchanges between Jesus and the Pharisees, Sadducees and
"chief priests." Rabbinic literature mentions Jesus occasionally, but
what the rabbis presume to know of him is derived from what they
heard or what they supposed the gospels or Christian missionaries were
saying, incorrectly comprehended or adapted by the rabbis themselves. [2]
Certainly, in rabbinic literature we have neither a reliable confirmation
nor an independent witness of Jesus' relations with any of the Jewish
leadership groups mentioned in the gospels.

Since it is thus on the Evangelists alone that we depend for our
knowledge of Jesus' specific controversies with Jewish leaders, the
Evangelists' understanding of these groups may be of more critical
importance than ours. Should they or their sources have misconstrued
the identity or nature of any of these authorities, or not really cared
for precision in presenting them, then our sole testimony concerning
Jesus' confrontations with these groups is of questionable reliability.

The gospels' descriptions are undoubtedly inadequate. The Synoptic
Gospels tend simply to present the various Jewish leadership groups
without clearly identifying them [3] or fully setting forth their roles
in society, [4] and, in some cases, without clearly distinguishing them
from one another by any criteria other than their differing names. [5]
It is not simply that we moderns have lost contact with who these
groups were, and hence must try to restore what the Evangelists felt
no need to include for us. Rather, the Evangelists themselves seem
unsure who all these groups were: hence their inadequacy in portraying
them. We do not know who "Herodians" were; must we presume
that the Evangelists *did* [6]—or that they, any better than we, could
distinguish between the scribes and Pharisees?

---

of the passage usually adopt one of three major positions: the passage is wholly an
interpolation; Josephus did include a less adulatory description of Jesus which was
later rendered more adulatory; Josephus did include a highly disparaging description of
Jesus whose tenor was later entirely changed.

[2] Some major treatments of these passages include those by R. T. Herford,
Christianity in Talmud and Midrash, London, 1903; J. Klausner, *Jesus of Nazareth*,
trans. H. Danby, repr., New York, 1943, 17-54; M. Goldstein, *Jesus in the Jewish
Tradition*, New York, 1950; J. Z. Lauterbach, "Jesus in the Talmud," *Rabbinic
Essays*, Cincinnati, 1951, 471-570. See also the survey of scholarship in D. R. Catchpole, *The Trial of Jesus: A Study in the Gospels and Jewish Historiography from
1770 to the Present Day*, Leiden, 1971, 1-71.

[3] As, e.g., in the case of Herodians or scribes.

[4] E.g., elders.

[5] E.g., scribes and Pharisees.

[6] See especially F. C. Grant, *The Earliest Gospel*, New York, 1943, 232; cf. S.
Sandmel, "Herodians," *IDB*, II, 594-595.

Moreover, why assume the group titles were intended to convey exactitude? The early Christian concern was to communicate not the identity of Jewish social or political groupings but the identity of Jesus as the Christ! Some of the group titles in the gospels were likely only general constructs, i.e., literary devices created and utilized for the narrators' convenience; they were hardly technical terms reflective of specific groups operative in Jesus' time or ever. Why struggle to identify exactly who the "Herodians" [7] or the "chief priests" [8] were —by recourse to gospel allusions, the Book of Acts, Josephus, rabbinic or apocalyptic-pseudepigraphic literature—when the Evangelists themselves may have given the matter far less thought and care than we?!

How likely it is that by "chief priests" the Evangelists meant just that: not any precisely delimited group but simply (and conveniently) the "more important" priests. The term need have no technical import at all. Did the developing Christian tradition have any need to preserve or convey precise definitions of the various components of the Judaean priestly structure? By the time the Evangelists themselves wrote, after 70 C.E., priests and Sadducees had ceased to be in the public eye anyway. Even though the Jewish rebellion of 66-73 may indeed have served to focus the eyes of Roman readers on the Temple and the priestly officialdom, [9] the vague term "chief priests," even as used in an early stratum of the Passion narrative, [10] could reflect the developing tradition's unfamiliarity with the priesthood rather than some precise acquaintance or even interest in it!

Consider the amorphous term "elders"! Are we to presume a well-defined socio-political grouping with this title? Need we invest time researching who they "were"? And how shall we approach "scribes," "Pharisees" and "Sadducees"? We cannot cavalierly dismiss *these* titles; "scribes," "Pharisees," "Sadducees" cannot be mere constructs

---

[7] Cf. B. W. Bacon, "Pharisees and Herodians in Mark," *JBL* 39 (1920), 102-112; F. J. Foakes-Jackson and K. Lake, *The Beginnings of Christianity*, I, London, 1920, 119-120; T. K. Cheyne, "Herodians," *EB*, II, Col. 2043; Taylor, *op. cit.*, 224; H. H. Rowley, "The Herodians in the Gospels," *JTS*, 41 (1940), 14-27; Branscomb, *op. cit.*, 61, 212; P. Winter, *On the Trial of Jesus*, Berlin, 1961, 128f., 210 n. 27; W. J. Bennett, Jr., "The Herodians of Mark's Gospel," *NovT* 17 (1975), 9-14.

[8] See attempts by E. Schürer, *A History of the Jewish People in the Time of Jesus Christ*, Edinburgh, 1885-1890, II, 1, 203-206; J. Jeremias, *Jerusalem in the Time of Jesus*, trans. F. H. and C. H. Cave, Philadelphia, 1969, 175-179; A. Guttmann, "The End of the Jewish Sacrificial Cult," *HUCA*, 38 (1967), 141ff.

[9] See especially Brandon, *Zealots*, 228ff.

[10] See Chapter Four.

because non-Christian sources actually mention them. Nevertheless, if the Evangelists may have cared so little for precision in their use of "elders," "Herodians" and "chief priests," let us anticipate a possible imprecision in their use of "scribes," "Pharisees" and "Sadducees." [11]

Methodologically speaking, it is appropriate to begin not with who the Jewish leadership groups are to us but with who they are to the Evangelists.

The Implications of Matthew's and Luke's Dependence on Mark for their Portrayal of Certain Jewish Leadership Groups

To what extent do Matthew and Luke depend on Mark for their portrayal of scribes, Pharisees and other Jewish leadership groups? We submit they depend heavily if not totally on Mark. Q is a hypothesis; we do not possess "Q" or other sources which allegedly underlie Matthaean or Lukan tradition. There is no way of demonstrating that the titles of Jewish authority groups actually appeared in sources such as Q, or even that there ever was a Q.

Since all the Synoptic Gospels are basically similar in their descriptions of the various Jewish leadership groups, many scholars—in attempting to define and distinguish each group—have recourse to all of the Synoptists, ignoring the probability of literary dependency. [12] This procedure is hardly sound. First we should ascertain the degree to which Mark's understanding of these groups is determinative of the comprehension (or non-comprehension) of them by the later Evangelists. If the Matthaean and Lukan portrayal is essentially only the preservation and embellishment of the Markan account, [13] then how justify recourse to Matthew and Luke in defining the Jewish leadership groups?

---

[11] On "scribes," e.g., note Riddle, op. cit., 102: "The other [i.e., other than "Herodians"] conventional identification of Mark, 'certain of the scribes who came down from Jerusalem,' similarly seems to be an attempt to secure verisimilitude by the use of restrictive terminology. Of course Mark's penchant for the term 'scribe' is a part of the phenomena of his scheme; it is not only difficult to invest the term with sufficient meaning in its frequent occurrences, but its use, especially in connection with other group names, in the passion story, ceases to have exact signification."

[12] This tendency is so widespread as to defy enumeration. For particularly clear examples, see A. T. Robertson, The Pharisees and Jesus, New York, 1920; A. T. Olmstead, Jesus in the Light of History, New York, 1942; A. Finkel, The Pharisees and the Teacher of Nazareth, Leiden, 1964; also Jeremias, op. cit., who, in his chapter on scribes and appendix on Pharisees, skips from one Synoptic Gospel to another, with many citations also from Acts.

For example, in attempting to define "Herodians," note the following instance:

MATTHEW	MARK	LUKE
12:14 But the Pharisees went out and took counsel against him, how to destroy him.	3:6 The Pharisees went out, and immediately held counsel with *the Herodians* against him, how to destroy him.	6:11 But they [the scribes and Pharisees] were filled with fury and discussed with one another what they might do to Jesus.

Here, Matthew (and Luke along with him) simply omits Herodians from Mark 3:6 so that, whereas in Mark, the Pharisees go out to take counsel against Jesus with the Herodians, in Matthew they take counsel among *themselves*! Examine the following as well:

MATTHEW	MARK	LUKE
16:6 Jesus said to them, "Take heed and beware of the leaven of the Pharisees and *Sadducees.*"	8:15 And he cautioned them saying, "Take heed, beware of the leaven of the Pharisees and the leaven of *Herod* [variant: of *the Herodians*]."	12:1 ...he began to say to his disciples first, "Beware of the leaven of the Pharisees, *which is hypocrisy.*"

Whether or not Mark has acquaintance with Herodians and Sadducees, he surely distinguishes between them; [14] here, however, Matthew *replaces* Herodians [15] with Sadducees. This is not necessarily because he equates the two; rather, he possibly cannot determine from the Markan account either who Herodians are or why they are present in this particular passage, and feels more comfortable substituting Sad-

---

[13] Any Lukan dependence on Matthew should, in this case, be construed dependence on Mark. See Chapter One, note 2.

[14] Mk. 12:13-27, mentioning both groups, in no way hints that they are closely or at all related.

[15] "Herodians" appear in Mk. 3:6 and 12:13. By analogy to 3:6 and 12:13, where Pharisees are bracketed with "Herodians," "Herod" in 8:15 should perhaps be understood as "Herodians," and a few texts read such. See Bacon, *art. cit.*, 104; A. T. Cadoux, *The Sources of the Second Gospel*, New York, 1935, 32, 158; Klausner, *op. cit.*, 297. Some regard "the leaven of Herod" as an addition to the passage whose purpose would be to bring 8:15 into conformity with 3:6. See Bacon, *The Beginnings of Gospel Story*, New Haven, 1909, 97.

ducees instead. [16] Mark is apparently Matthew's sole source for Herodians; where Mark fails to assist him, Matthew is left dangling and has to take other measures. [17]

Luke, meanwhile, follows Matthew's lead in the former instance by dropping Herodians. [18] Luke as well as Matthew depends upon Mark for acquaintance with Herodians and, discerning Matthew's "bewilderment," Luke himself then comes to share it. In the second example, however, he omits not only Mark's Herod(ians) but Matthew's Sadducees as well. Since Luke is sensitive to tensions between Pharisees and Sadducees, [19] Matthew's casual substitution of Sadducees for Herodians may have struck Luke as infelicitous: one could infer from Matthew's rendition a too quick association of two groups whom Luke knows (possibly from Josephus [20]) were continuously at odds with one another. Luke winnows out Mark's Herodians because, like Matthew, he does not know who they are, and also omits Matthew's Sadducees because they are in context inappropriate as a replacement; instead, Luke merely adjusts his text so as to read "the leaven of the Pharisees,

---

[16] Most likely, Matthew understands "leaven" to mean "teaching" (cf. 16:11-12), but cannot fathom how Mark can characterize Herod (or Herodians) as the source of "teachings."

[17] Matthew does mention Herodians in 22:16, likely the result of inadvertent copying (W. L. Knox, *The Sources of the Synoptic Gospels: Vol. I St. Mark*, Cambridge, 1953, 9-10, 57 n. 1). The context of this particular passage is such that Matthew could comfortably reproduce Mark's "Herodians" even without knowing who they were. Luke, however, in 20:20, drops Herodians from Matthew, possibly substituting "the governor" for them, especially if by "the governor" he means Herod Antipas (cf. Lk. 23:7).

[18] Knox, *ibid.*, suggests that Matthew and Luke dropped the term either because they felt it was meaningless to their readers or because it was meaningless to them themselves (cf. also S. MacLean Gilmour, "St. Luke," *IB*, VIII, 350). Moreover, he feels Mark himself did not know who the Herodians were either. Grant, *Earliest Gospel*, 232, agrees. Whether or not the term had some meaning for Mark, indications are that it was not supplied by Mark himself (since he seems so unsure who they were) but rather was lifted by him from an earlier written collection of controversy pericopae involving Pharisees and Herodians, stressing the former. Burkill comments: "...it is not impossible that the similar stories of xii, 13-44 were derived from the same (written) source [as that underlying ii, 1-iii, 6], for iii, 6 and xii, 13 are the only passages in the work which mention the Herodians ("Anti-Semitism in St. Mark's Gospel," *NovT* 3 [1959], 39, n. 2; also in French, "L'antisémitisme dans l'évangile selon Saint Marc," *RHR* 154 [1958], 16 n. 1).

[19] See Acts 23:6-8.

[20] On the problem of Luke's possible familiarity with Josephus' writings, including *Antiquities*, see M. Krenkel, *Josephus und Lucas*, Leipzig, 1894; cf. J. Moffatt, *op. cit.*, 29-31; Foakes-Jackson and Lake, *op. cit.*, II, 357 and IV, 276f.; Enslin, *Christian Beginnings*, 422-424; H. W. Montefiore, *Josephus and the New Testament*, London, 1962 (from *NovT* IV, Fasc. 2 & 4 [1960]).

which is hypocrisy." Conceivably, Matthew's very willingness to bracket Pharisees with Sadducees [21] reflects his own unfamiliarity with Sadducees as well as Herodians. [22] We believe Mark is his only source on Sadducees as well as Herodians; and since Mark (or *his* source) in 12:28 designates the Sadducees' opponent as a "scribe" rather than a "Pharisee," Matthew may not have been as sensitive as Luke to the tensions between Sadducees and Pharisees.

Matthew's comprehension of scribes is a matter of far more consequence than his problems with Herodians—for "scribes" (or "scribe") are the most frequently mentioned group in Mark, appearing twenty-one times. [23] Matthew seems perplexed by "scribes." In distinguishing scribes from Pharisees, he could have wished for Mark's assistance, but Mark offers none! In virtually all respects, the scribes and Pharisees in Mark appear similar, practically identical: *both* are groups of teachers, evidently interpreters of Jewish law and its ritual implementation; and both uphold the tradition of the elders. [24] *Jointly*, they harass and badger Jesus regarding observance of the Law. [25] *Each* group appears both in Galilee *and* in Judaea. [26] The scribal stance toward the Sadducees is precisely Pharisaic. [27] Both scribes and Pharisees are allegedly disaffected with the plight of the unfortunate sinner. [28] Moreover, Jesus views both groups in similar terms: they are hypocritical, blind and deceitful. [29] Each group is involved in conspiracy against Jesus. [30]

In the forthcoming argument, we only intend to raise a conjecture. We cannot prove that we are correct; indeed, there is even a circular

---

[21] See Mt. 16:1.

[22] Matthew mentions Sadducees seven times. On two of these occasions, he is clearly basing himself on what he finds in Mark's sole mention of Sadducees (Mt. 22:23, 34; cf. Mk. 12:18-27). On the remaining five occasions, each time Sadducees appear bracketed with Pharisees (Mt. 3:7; 16:1, 6, 11, 12). *Bracketing* is a device Matthew frequently employs, especially when he is puzzled as to the exact identity of a leadership group, as we shall demonstrate shortly.

[23] Mk. 1:22; 2:6, 16; 3:22; 7:1, 5; 8:31; 9:11, 14; 10:33; 11:18, 27; 12:28, 32, 35, 38; 14:1, 43, 53; 15:1, 31.

[24] E.g., Mk. 7:5, 8, 9, 13.

[25] Mk. 7:1, 5; cf. 2:16.

[26] Scribes appear to come from Jerusalem into Galilee (e.g., 3:22; 7:1), while Pharisees seem to be present in both Galilee and Judaea (2:18f.; 7:1f.; 10:1f.; 12:13f.).

[27] Mk. 12:18-28.

[28] Mk. 2:16ff.

[29] Mk. 7:1ff.

[30] The Pharisees plot his destruction, as in Mk. 3:6; the scribes in 14:1 and subsequent passages of the Passion narrative; cf. 8:31; 10:33; 11:18, 27.

dimension to our reasoning. Our sole concern is to present plausible grounds for *suspecting* that Matthew was unfamiliar with "scribes." If Matthew wished to include scribes in his Gospel, and—as just indicated—it was unclear to him on the basis of Mark who they were, then what options were open to him?

a) He might bracket scribes with Pharisees wherever possible; since, on the basis of Mark, the two groups emerge as virtually indistinguishable, Matthew could safely juxtapose scribes with Pharisees so that they partake of the same activities jointly.

b) He might replace Mark's scribes with the apparently identical Pharisees (the latter term possibly being more familiar in Matthew's day).

c) He might simply omit scribes whenever possible (a procedure most easily accomplished where Markan scribes appear in combination with other groups rather than by themselves, these other groups continuing to support the story line).

Let it be observed that Matthew follows precisely these procedures:

a) In ten [31] of his twenty-three mentions of scribes, Matthew *juxtaposes scribes with Pharisees*, particularly in Chapter 23. It is unnecessary to ascribe this bracketing of "scribes" and "Pharisees" to Q [32] or any special Matthaean source; it could simply derive from Matthew's inability to understand from Mark's Gospel how scribes and Pharisees differ, and from Matthew's attempt to camouflage this inability.

Matthew 23 presents us with the extremely peculiar circumstance: a whole stream of specific denunciations and accusations hurled at two supposedly distinct groups of persons who, for some inexplicable reason, seem in every way identical! Not one but both groups sit on Moses' chair. They both love the best seats in the synagogue, they both (?) are called "Rabbi," they both traverse sea and land to make one proselyte, they both tithe mint and dill and cummin and strain out a gnat and swallow a camel, they both cleanse the outside of the plate, they both are like white-washed tombs, they both build the tombs of the prophets, and they both either "kill" or "crucify" or "scourge" or "persecute" "prophets and wise men and scribes [!]," and so on

---

[31] Mt. 5:20; 12:38; 15:1; 23:2, 13, 15, 23, 25, 27, 29.

[32] In such a case, the logia would presumably have preserved not only the sayings but also both titles of the groups addressed, as in *"scribes, Pharisees,* hypocrites!"

and so forth. Indeed, remarkably enough, on the one occasion when Mark actually hints how scribes and Pharisees differ, Matthew obliterates the distinction! [33]

How puzzled is the reader who wonders: Have the scribes no shortcoming *unique* to themselves? Must they always duplicate the Pharisees? [34] Surely our puzzlement with Matthew is rooted in Matthew's puzzlement with Mark! Matthew seems not to know who scribes are, and Mark, his only source, leaves him distinctly uninformed.

b) Notice, moreover, how readily Matthew adjusts Mark by *replacing scribes with Pharisees*:

MARK	MATTHEW
3:22 And *the scribes* who came down from Jerusalem said....	9:34 But *the Pharisees* said....
12:28 And *one of the scribes* came up and heard them disputing with one another, and seeing that he answered them well, asked him,...	22:34-35 But when *the Pharisees* heard that he had silenced the Sadducees, they came together. And *one of them*, a lawyer, [35] asked him a question, to test him.
12:35 And as Jesus taught in the temple, he said, "How can *the scribes* say that the Christ is the son of David?"...	22:41 Now while *the Pharisees* were gathered together, Jesus asked them a question, saying....

Earlier, we suggested that Matthew substituted "Sadducees" for "Herodians" in 16:6 (cf. Mk. 8:15) because of uncertainty as to the Herodians' identity and activity. Similarly, in the three examples just cited, he substitutes "Pharisees" for "scribes." Since Mark himself fails to distinguish between the two groups, Matthew freely replaces "scribes,"

---

[33]

MARK	MATTHEW
7:1 Now when the Pharisees gathered together to him, with some of the scribes, who had come from Jerusalem, ...	15:1 Then Pharisees and scribes came to Jesus from Jerusalem....

Whereas Mark implies that the Pharisees are native to Galilee (at least *these* particular Pharisees), with the scribes being residents of Jerusalem who travel into Galilee (at least *these* scribes), Matthew obliterates any distinction by having the Pharisees also come from Jerusalem! See Taylor, *op. cit.*, 334-335.

[34] Jeremias, *op. cit.*, 252-253, also observes that scribes and Pharisees become confused with one another: "...Matthew and Luke very often lump together 'the Scribes and Pharisees'.... On the other hand Mark and John do not.... Matthew ... thereby obliterates the difference between the two groups...." But Jeremias is unable to account for *why* Matthew is prompted to do so.

[35] "Lawyer" is to be understood here as one of the Pharisees, not a member of another leadership group.

whom he does not comprehend, with "Pharisees," with whom he is more familiar and hence more comfortable.

c) Meanwhile, in many other instances, Matthew *omits Markan scribes altogether,* [36] without replacing them with Pharisees. Since he does not comprehend who scribes are, he simply drops them where convenient (precisely as he does in the case of Herodians in 12:14 [cf. Mk. 3:6]):

MARK	MATTHEW
2:16 And *the scribes* of the Pharisees [or the variant: and *the scribes* and the Pharisees]....	9:11 And when the Pharisees saw this....
9:14 And when they came to the disciples, they saw a great crowd about them, and *scribes* arguing with them.	17:14 And when they came to the crowd, a man came....
11:27 ...And as he was walking in the temple, the chief priests and *the scribes* and the elders came to him.	21:23 And when he entered the temple, the chief priests and the elders of the people came up to him....
14:1 And the chief priests and *the scribes* were seeking how to arrest him by stealth....	26:3 Then the chief priests and the elders of the people gathered, ... and took counsel together in order to arrest Jesus by stealth.... (Here the deletion of "scribes" is effected by substitution of "elders of the people.")
14:43 And immediately, while he was still speaking, Judas came, ... and with him a crowd ... from the chief priests and *the scribes* and the elders.	26:47 Judas came, ... and with him a great crowd ... from the chief priests and the elders of the people.
15:1 And as soon as it was morning the chief priests, with the elders and *scribes,* ... held a consultation....	27:1 When morning came, all the chief priests and the elders of the people took counsel against Jesus to put him to death.

On the basis of this analysis, we offer the following observations:

1. Matthew omits more than half of Mark's twenty-one references to scribes. [37]

---

[36] See G. Sloyan, *Jesus on Trial*, Philadelphia, 1973, 76, 130.

[37] The following eleven have been omitted: Mk. 2:16; 3:22; 7:5; 9:14; 11:27; 12:28, 32; 12:35; 14:1; 14:43; 15:1. The omissions are accomplished either by simple deletion of the term "scribes" only (cf. Mk. 2:16 with Mt. 9:11; Mk. 11:27 with Mt. 21:23; Mk. 14:1 with Mt. 26:3; Mk. 14:43 with Mt. 26:47; Mk. 15:1 with Mt. 27:1), or by deletion of the clauses in which "scribes" appear (cf. Mk. 9:14

2. Of the remaining ten mentions, which Matthew retains, in six the scribes are bracketed with one or more other groups, and do not in these six appear alone in Matthew. [38]

3. Of the remaining four, in one [39] Matthew makes scribes part of a combination with Pharisees. [40]

4. In one [41] of the three remaining passages, Matthew changes "the scribes" to "their scribes," and in a second passage [42] the scribes are mentioned by the disciples but are not themselves present.

Only once [43] out of twenty-one times does Matthew reproduce a Markan reference to scribes in a manner implying that Matthew knows who they are—and such a reproduction could result from mere copying! Moreover, not even here does Matthew indicate who the scribes are, [44] but, then, neither does Mark!

Moreover, there are thirteen instances wherein Matthew mentions scribes in material found in Matthew but not in Mark. But in ten of these thirteen instances, scribes are not mentioned alone but are bracketed with other groups. [45] One remaining mention of scribes is of a group undefined altogether and obviously distinct from the kind of scribes whom we are examining; [46] and the two other mentions of scribes are only of "scribe" in the singular, possibly unrelated to the "scribes" under discussion. [47] There are, then, grounds for suspecting that Matthew is not himself familiar with the identity of the "scribes" and that he relies totally on Mark in this respect.

---

with Mt. 17:14; Mk. 7:5 with Mt. 15:1; Mk. 12:32 with Mt. 12:40f.), or by replacing "scribes" with "Pharisees" (cf. Mk. 3:22 with Mt. 9:34 and 12:24; Mk. 12:28 with Mt. 22:34-35; Mk. 12:35 with Mt. 22:41).

[38] See Mk. 7:1 and Mt. 15:1; Mk. 8:31 and Mt. 16:21; Mk. 10:33 and Mt. 20:18; Mk. 11:18 and Mt. 21:15; Mk. 14:53 and Mt. 26:57; Mk. 15:31 and Mt. 27:41.

[39] Mk. 12:38.

[40] Mt. 23:13, 15, 23, 25, 27, 29 and most likely also 23:2 and 5:20 could have been inspired by Mk. 12:38ff. Cf. Kee, op. cit., 149.

[41] Mk. 1:22; cf. Mt. 7:29.

[42] Mk. 9:11; cf. Mt. 17:10.

[43] Mk. 2:6; cf. Mt. 9:3.

[44] Perhaps he is relying on his previous mention of them, 7:29, to clarify their identity, but he never explains who they are in 7:29 either!

[45] With chief priests: Mt. 2:4; with Pharisees: 5:20; 12:38; 23:2, 13, 15, 23, 25, 27, 29.

[46] Mt. 23:34; see A. F. J. Klijn, "Scribes, Pharisees, High Priests and Elders in the New Testament," NovT 3 (1959), 262-263, and his reference to Klostermann in 263 note 1.

[47] Mt. 8:19 and 13:52. On the latter, see references in ibid., 263 note 4. In these passages, it is not clear that we are dealing with Jewish groups.

An examination of Luke reveals more of the same: he also does not clearly distinguish Pharisees and scribes. [48] But he does define what they have in common, inferring from the way they are treated in Mark (and perhaps also in Matthew—if Luke had Matthew to consult) that scribes and Pharisees are a kind of "lawyers" or "teachers of the Law." [49]

Matthew himself once suggests that the Pharisees are lawyers. [50] Moreover, Josephus (to whose works, we have already suggested, Luke may have had access) emphasizes the Pharisees as interpreters of the Law. [51] Not specifying how scribes differ from Pharisees, Luke defines what they have in common, applying the same terms, "lawyers" and "teachers of the Law," to the seemingly identical scribes and Pharisees. But the rapid reader could misconstrue "lawyers" and "teachers of the Law" to represent *additional* Jewish leadership groups; instead of only "scribes" and "Pharisees," the groups would be four: "scribes," "Pharisees," "lawyers" and "teachers of the Law." [52]

The account of Paul's trial in Acts 23 may be instructive here. The device of a trial, wherein the Jewish protagonists are shown to be in error, and wherein the defendant is ultimately adjudged innocent and emerges with dignity in the eyes of Rome, is employed in both volumes of Luke-Acts, first in the case of Jesus, and subsequently in the case of Paul. What interests us here is the issue of resurrection as it surfaces in the account of Paul's trial. We would like to know why Luke represents the Sadducees' opponents here as Pharisees when, in Mark, a Lukan source, the Sadducees' opponent on the issue of resurrection is the scribe. Note the parallelism here:

---

[48] See, e.g., Lk. 11:43 together with 20:46.

[49] See Taylor, *op. cit.*, 173. Examples of Luke's use of lawyers and teachers of the Law where Matthew or Mark uses scribes and/or Pharisees are the following: Mt. 23:4 and Lk. 11:46; Mt. 23:13 and Lk. 11:52; Mk. 12:28 and Lk. 10:25; Mk. 2:6 and Mt. 9:3 and Lk. 5:17, 21.

[50] Mt. 22:34-35.

[51] *War* I.v.2 (i.110); *Antiquities* XIII.x.6 (xiii.297); XVII.ii.4 (xvii.41); *Life* 38 (191).

[52] Even as he clarifies and defines, Luke tends to confuse. Sometimes, he presents "lawyers" or "teachers of the Law" as applying solely to one group (scribes *or* Pharisees)—as if to reserve the appropriateness of the term for the one group and to deny it to the other; and yet, elsewhere, he may apply the same term to the *other* group instead! Thus, e.g., while in Mk. 2:1-12 only scribes are present, the parallel, Luke 5:17, tells that "there were Pharisees and teachers of the Law sitting by." Four verses later, in Lk. 5:21, the same Pharisees are bracketed with scribes, so that we could conclude Luke evidently regards *scribes but not Pharisees* as here being teachers of the Law. But later, in Acts 5:33-34, Luke describes Gamaliel *the Pharisee* as a "teacher of the Law."

	MARK 12	ACTS 23
Religious issue involved	Resurrection	Resurrection
Those denying resurrection	Sadducees	Sadducees
Those affirming resurrection	Jesus +	Paul +
	scribe(s)	Pharisees (vv. 6-8)
		or "scribes of the
		Pharisees' party" (v. 9)

Possibly, Luke himself has perceived the Pharisaic character of the scribe in Mark 12:28ff. Conceivably also, however, Luke was led to this perception through Josephus who indicates very clearly that resurrection was a key point of contention (not between the Sadducees and the *scribes*, whom Josephus never mentions in this context but) between the Sadducees and the *Pharisees*. [53] In such a case, since Mark, in Chapter 12, casts a scribe in the Pharisaic role in the resurrection dispute, Luke inferred that scribes were identical with Pharisees, and then proceeded to describe both groups as "lawyers" or "teachers of the Law." We believe the peculiar phrase in Acts 23:9, "the scribes of the Pharisees' party," arises from Luke's retention of Mark's "scribe" [54] from 12:28 and Mark's "the scribes of [*or* and] the Pharisees" from 2:16 plus Luke's understanding from Josephus that the Sadducees' opponents on resurrection were the "Pharisees." [55]

In sum, therefore, we have detected indications that the manner in which certain Jewish leadership groups are depicted in Matthew and Luke could reflect Matthew's dependence on Mark alone, and Luke's utilization of Matthew and Josephus as well as Mark. The fundamental consideration that this is *possible* methodologically requires that the study of Jewish leadership groups in the gospels be made initially within the confines of Mark alone; hence the concentration of this volume on Mark and the deliberate limit in consulting Matthew and Luke to clarify the Markan descriptions of scribes and Pharisees and other groups in their relations with Jesus. [56]

---

[53] *War* II.viii.14 (ii.162-166); *Antiquities* XVIII.i.3-4 (xviii.12-17).

[54] Perhaps Mk. 12:18-27 was in origin a scribe vs. Sadducee (or a Pharisee vs. Sadducee) argument over resurrection; initially, Jesus was not part of the tradition but later came to replace the scribes/Pharisees since he was aligned with them on the issue of resurrection. Notice of their alignment is preserved by the approval of the scribe in 12:28.

[55] Cf. *supra*, n. 20. We discuss this problem at greater length in Chapter Five.

[56] A particularly useful study of the mentions of Jewish leadership groups in the Synoptic Gospels is that by A. F. J. Klijn, *art. cit.*, 259-267. Though he has different concerns in mind, he also demonstrates how "the synoptic gospels show a remarkable disagreement in parallel passages dealing with these groups," and he attempts to plot therefrom a possible development in the tradition regarding these groups.

The Degree of Mark's Dependence on His Sources for His Familiarity
with Jewish Leadership Groups

If Matthew's and Luke's imprecisions and seeming confusions may
be traced to their dependence on Mark, how then explain Mark's own
uncertainties? Were these a function of *his* dependence on sources?
Not all Mark's mentions of Jewish leadership groups were necessarily
derived from his sources; as we shall demonstrate later, in some
pericopae he himself introduces the group titles. Nevertheless, we
would contend that Mark was as much dependent on his sources as
Matthew and Luke were dependent on him.

That Mark was somewhat familiar with Pharisees is likely, especially
given his interpolation in the verses 7:3-4; as we shall discuss in the
succeeding chapter, they were the one group flourishing after 70 C.E.,
when Mark seems to have written, and widespread in the Diaspora,
where Mark seems to have lived. Following 70 C.E., the other terms
—scribes, elders, Herodians, Sadducees and chief priests—may have
had very little currency. Mark's familiarity with *these* groups must have
come from elsewhere than personal acquaintance. We shall set forth
that he lifted information from three written sources and then improvised extensively. We will now advance data and argument supportive of this position.

CHAPTER THREE

TWO PRE-MARKAN CONTROVERSY COLLECTIONS

Why Two Camps of Conspirators in Mark?

While Mark alleges that five Jewish leadership groups shared a desire to have Jesus arrested and executed, he appears to compartmentalize them into two separate camps:

1. Chief priests + scribes + elders; [1]
2. Pharisees + Herodians. [2]

Instead of joining forces, these two sets of conspirators have no contact or communication with one another except when scribes and Pharisees are conjoined in 7:1, 5 (cf. 2:16). [3] Never in their fourteen appearances [4] do chief priests, in the one camp, encounter, much less conspire with, either Pharisees [5] or Herodians [6] in the other camp; elders never meet them either; [7] in twenty-one appearances, [8] scribes are never mentioned with Herodians, and, aside from the exceptions noted, not with Pharisees either. [9]

---

[1] Chief priests, scribes and elders are conjoined in the following passages: 8:31; 11:27; 14:43, 53; 15:1. Sometimes, only the chief priests and the scribes are present: 10:33; 11:18; 14:1; 15:31.

[2] Pharisees and Herodians are conjoined in 3:6 and 12:13 (and possibly in 8:15; see Chapter Two, note 15).

[3] The exact reading in 7:1 is "certain of the scribes." The variant reading in 2:16 is "the scribes *and* the Pharisees"; on the problem see Burkill, *New Light*, 223 n. 56; Bacon, *Beginnings*, 28-29; Dibelius, *op. cit.*, 64; Taylor, *op. cit.*, 173, 206, 209.

[4] 8:31; 10:33; 11:18, 27; 14:1, 10, 43, 53, 55; 15:1, 3, 10, 11, 31.

[5] Chief priests never appear in any of the eleven mentions of Pharisees: 2:16, 18, 24; 3:6; 7:1, 3, 5; 8:11, 15; 10:2; 12:13.

[6] Chief priests are not present when Herodians appear; see 3:6 and 12:13; cf. 8:15.

[7] Elders are mentioned five times: 8:31; 11:27; 14:43, 53; 15:1. They never appear with Pharisees or Herodians. The word "elders" does appear twice, however, in 7:1ff., a passage mentioning Pharisees. Yet here the term "elders" does not connote the specific leadership group we know from the Passion narrative, but rather simply "generations of teachers."

[8] 1:22; 2:6, 16; 3:22, 7:1, 5; 8:31; 9:11, 14; 10:33; 11:18, 27; 12:28, 32, 35, 38; 14:1, 43, 53; 15:1, 31.

[9] The Sadducees are included in neither of the two conspiratorial camps. As a matter of fact, they appear only once, in 12:18ff. Compared to the other leadership groups, then, the Sadducees are insignificant to Mark; it is only their view on resurrection which accounts for their inclusion here. They take no part in any conspiracy against Jesus.

While the two camps thus appear radically segregated from each other, within each camp some allies are rigidly bound to others. Herodians never act or appear independently—their partners, the Pharisees, are always bracketed with them; [10] whenever elders are mentioned, one can be sure their fellows, the chief priests, will be mentioned in the same breath, and the scribes as well. [11] Not even the powerful chief priests manage to appear alone; nine times they are bracketed with one or both of their usual allies, scribes or elders, and the five instances when they seem independent are only illusory. [12]

We propose to examine this pattern of rigid compartmentalization and the occasional departures from it, and to test the following hypothesis: that this redactional scheme derives from Mark's utilization of three sources for his knowledge of Jewish leadership groups, and that Mark's departures from this scheme result from his attempts to accommodate these three sources to one another and to his larger redactional aims. We acknowledge at the outset that our thesis cannot be fully

---

[10] See 3:6; 12:13; cf. 8:15. The account of Herod Antipas in 6:14-28 does not involve Herodians in the sense pertinent here.

[11] See 8:31; 11:27; 14:43, 53; 15:1.

[12] Cf. note 4. The five passages when they are mentioned independently are: 14:10, 55; 15:3, 10, 11. In all likelihood, however, 14:10f. was originally a continuation of 14:1-2, with verses 3-9 being inserted or interwoven; the chief priests in verse 10, therefore, are still working in concert with the scribes from verses 1-2. See R. Bultmann, *The History of the Synoptic Tradition*, trans. J. Marsh, Oxford, 1963, 262f.; Dibelius, *op. cit.*, 181, 186, 205; W. L. Knox, *op. cit.*, 117f.; cf. citations of G. Schille, Dibelius and Taylor by Donahue, "Introduction: From Passion Traditions to Passion Narrative," in *The Passion in Mark: Studies on Mark 14-16*, ed. W. H. Kelber, Philadelphia, 1976, 7ff.; also V. K. Robbins, "Last Meal: Preparation, Betrayal, and Absence (Mark 14:12-25)," *ibid.*, 29n. In 14:55, meanwhile, the chief priests are actually still joined with "the elders and the scribes" mentioned in 14:53; for in verse 55, the chief priests are bracketed with "the whole council," evidently a reference to their usual partners mentioned just earlier. (Admittedly, in 15:1, the "council" seems distinct from the scribes and elders; one could therefore argue that, in 14:55, scribes and elders are absent and chief priests really do appear alone. But verse 55 begins a section considered by some scholars an interpolation and we fully agree. Cf. especially Donahue, "Temple, Trial, and Royal Christology: [Mark 14:53-65]," *ibid.*, 61-79. Verse 55 should thus be seen as a loosely constructed transition between verse 53 and the trial scene in the Sanhedrin. The "council" was introduced from 15:1. The earlier tradition is reflected in 14:53 and 15:1 [Donahue, *Are You the Christ?*, 65] where chief priests do not appear alone but are bracketed with their two usual allies. It could also be argued, moreover, that, since 14:55 was constructed so as to continue 14:53, it is legitimate to assume that the scribes and elders present in 14:53 are still present in 14:55, even though they are not there explicitly mentioned.) Similarly, 15:3 continues 15:1, so the scribes and elders from verse 1 are still in the chief priests' company in the appearance before Pilate in verse 3, and the same applies also to verses 10-11.

proved. This is a problem in virtually all studies in source criticism. Our aim is solely to present an idea and to demonstrate its plausibility. If our thesis is correct, then significant implications come to mind. In our concluding chapter, we shall indicate what these implications are.

M. Albertz' Theory of Two
Pre-Markan Controversy Collections

That some kind of source dependence underlies Mark's treatment of Jesus' opponents has long been alleged, on three bases. One, as we shall indicate in more detail shortly, various sections of his Gospel betray reliance on earlier written sources; the same may be true when it comes to material on the conspirators. Two, he was writing at a time when terms such as "chief priests," "scribes," "elders," "Herodians," were no longer current—the only leadership group prominent and widespread after 70 C.E. was the Pharisees/rabbis; especially if the author of Mark was himself a product of the Diaspora, a theory of source dependence would conveniently explain his seeming familiarity with groups of a former age and distant locale. Three, Markan pericopae presenting leadership groups tend to be clustered, [13] perhaps betraying Mark's incorporation of written sources either in chunks or fully intact.

The earliest notable study of this problem was by M. Albertz whose particular focus was on the sources for Mark's controversy traditions rather than for the leadership groups *per se*. [14] Relying on a number of criteria—including geographical differentiation and pericopae clusters—he posited two pre-Markan collections: One, he alleged, was set in Galilee, underlying the controversies between Jesus and a variety of opponents in 2:1-3:6; Mark incorporated this source virtually intact as he himself had received it. [15] The other collection, set in Jerusalem, can be detected beneath the dialogues in 11:15-12:40; [16] as we now

---

[13] Chief priests, scribes and elders are concentrated in the Passion narrative (Chapters 14-15) and in passages preparing us for it (8:31; 10:33; 11:18, 27); Chapter 12, meanwhile, contains a number of pericopae focusing on the scribes, with the bulk of Pharisee material bunched in 2:16-3:6 and 7:1ff.

[14] *Die synoptischen Streitgespräche*, Berlin, 1921. "Controversy stories," as defined by Kee (*op. cit.*, 187 n. 122) include "narratives concerning explicit controversies with scribes/Pharisees etc., sayings which reflect a controversy background, disputes over legal or interpretational issues and pronouncements against Jesus' opponents."

[15] See especially 5-16.

[16] See especially 16-36.

have it, however, this section contains pieces foreign to the original collection. [17]

With regard to the first pre-Markan collection, Albertz' position rests on the following arguments:

First, the peaking of the conflict between the Pharisees and Jesus in Mk. 3:6 ("the Pharisees went out, and immediately held counsel with the Herodians against him, how to destroy him") seems to be premature. As Albertz conceives of Mark's own literary plan, Jesus first indicates what his fate will be in Mk. 8:31. The foreshadowing of the Passion as early as Mk. 3:6 is untimely and unsatisfying. [18] How then explain Mk. 3:6? In answer, the passage originally concluded a pre-Markan collection, extending back to what is Mk. 2:1, and Mark incorporated the whole collection intact into his Gospel—not daring to remove the concluding verse despite its clash with his wider literary scheme. [19]

Second, hostility between Jesus and his opponents steadily escalates from Mk. 2:1 through 3:6, reaching a degree so intense in 3:6 that 3:22-30 constitutes an inexplicable letdown. In the exchange in 3:1-6, Jesus' behavior toward Jewish authorities incites them to revenge—they are already plotting his destruction. How distinctly unexpected and surprising it is, therefore, to find Jesus and the scribes in such a low-key exchange in 3:22ff.! Now if Mark himself had arranged 2:1-3:6—a cluster of controversies in an order of *increasing* tension [20]—how

---

[17] Mk. 11:18-26; 12:1-12.

[18] Luke himself (6:11) seems to have sensed this, toning down Mk. 3:6: "But they were filled with fury and discussed with one another what they might do to Jesus."

[19] The problem of Mk. 3:6 deserves considerable attention as we shall have occasion to refer to this verse in subsequent chapters. Bultmann holds that the original pericope consisted of 3:1-5; verse 6 would therefore be secondary, since in the opening verses "the opponents of Jesus are not described as Scribes or Pharisees, but are unspecified. It is only in the secondary v.6 that they are identified as Pharisees" (*op. cit.*, 52; cf. 63). But the question remains whether, if v.6 is secondary, it was Mark himself who added it (as, for example, is contended by Dibelius, *op. cit.*, 44-45) or whether it was itself a secondary verse incorporated by the compiler of the pre-Markan collection himself; cf. Burkill, "Anti-Semitism," 39 n. 2. Moreover, if a collector is involved, 3:1-5 would be naturally understood in conjunction with the preceding pericope, 2:23-28, such that the presence of at least the Pharisees would have been assumed all along. W. L. Knox agrees with Albertz that 3:6 was already present in the pre-Markan collection (*op. cit.*, 10 n. 2); so also does B. S. Easton, *The Gospel Before the Gospels*, New York, 1928, 71. Still other factors and options must be considered, however, particularly the appearance of Pharisees and Herodians in 12:13ff. and the possibility that this pericope on Tribute was originally sandwiched between 3:1-5 and 3:6.

[20] *Op. cit.*, pages 5-16. Albertz sketches out the *increasing* tension in the five

could he have tolerated such an abrupt diminution of this tension in 3:22-30? Albertz attempts to resolve this problem as follows: 2:1-3:6 must constitute a pre-Markan collection of controversy pericopae, arranged in escalating tension; Mark incorporated this collection *in toto.* Thereby Albertz explains the disharmony between 2:1-3:6, on the one hand, and 3:22ff., on the other.

Third, the expression "Son of man" appears twice in the section 2:1-3:6—in 2:10, 28. Since the term does not otherwise appear in Mark again until as late as 8:31 (the first prediction of the Passion), and from then on appears with increased frequency, its dual appearance in Mk. 2:1-3:6 is problematic. Albertz resolves this difficulty as he does the other two: 2:1-3:6 is a pre-Markan collection which happened to use "Son of man" twice, and this accounts for the premature appearance of the term before 8:31—where Mark himself preferred to begin using it. Moreover, the collection uses "Son of man" in a human rather than a supernatural sense. This definitely distinguishes the term's appearances in 2:1-3:6 from appearances in the second half of the Gospel, and implies that 2:1-3:6 is special material in the composition and arrangement of which Mark himself was not involved. [21]

---

episodes as follows: In the story of the paralytic, the hostility of the scribes is *kept to themselves:* "Now some of the scribes were sitting there, questioning in their hearts.... And ... Jesus, perceiving ... that they thus questioned within themselves...." In the succeeding pericope, the objection to Jesus is *audible,* but addressed *to the disciples* and not to Jesus himself: "And the scribes of the Pharisees ... said to his disciples, ... And when Jesus heard it, he said to them...." In the third episode, Jesus himself is questioned, but the query seeks clarification of the behavior of the *disciples* and not that of Jesus himself: "...and people came and said to him, 'Why do John's disciples and the disciples of the Pharisees fast, but your disciples do not fast?' And Jesus said to them...." In the fourth incident, again it is, strictly speaking, the disciples' behavior rather than Jesus' which is involved, yet the *tone* of the Pharisees' query is one of *accusation against Jesus himself*—he is responsible for his disciples' actions: "...And the Pharisees said to him, 'Look, why are they doing what is not lawful on the sabbath?' And he said to them, 'Have you never read what David did...?' " Finally, in the last story, *Jesus' own behavior* is implicitly condemned; his opponents are silent in the face of his questioning, and he—himself now emotionally wrought up— is revolted at their hardness of heart; and thereupon, in open enmity, the Pharisees go out to hold "counsel with the Herodians against him, how to destroy him." While E. Fascher agrees with Albertz, he cites Bultmann's view that the level of tension remains much the same throughout; see *Die formgeschichtliche Methode: eine Darstellung und Kritik,* Giessen, 1924, 147.

[21] Complicating the particular problem at hand are suspicions by some that the wider contexts in which "Son of man" appears (Mk. 2:5b-10; 2:27-28) in this proposed pre-Markan collection are themselves secondary and not of a piece with the material preceding them. Cf., on 2:5b-10, W. Bousset, *Kyrios Christos,* trans. J. E. Steely, Nashville, 1970, 77-78; Bultmann, *op. cit.,* 14-16; Branscomb, *op. cit.,* 43; E. Klostermann, *Das Markusevangelium,* 2d ed., Tübingen, 1926, *ad. loc.;* Bacon,

The contents of this first pre-Markan collection can be thought of as having gone through three phases: first, there existed individual stories; next, these stories were combined into a collection, capped by the closing verse 3:6; finally, certain verses (2:13, 17b, 19b-20, 21f., 27f.) were inserted, [22] and Mark incorporated the whole collection into his Gospel. And what purpose had this early collection been intended to serve? The original compiler had wished to explain how the hostility between Jesus and the Jewish authorities developed. Mark himself, sharing this concern, thus readily appropriated this material. [23]

Again, in the second collection posited by Albertz, there are at least five episodes: on Authority (Mk. 11:27-33); on Tribute to Caesar (12:13-17); on the Resurrection (12:18-27); on the First Commandment (12:28-34); and on David's Son (12:35-37), with an introduction in the story of the Cleansing of the Temple (11:15ff.) and a concluding warning against the scribes (12:38-40). Albertz feels the latter could have been added by Mark himself. These episodes are arranged topically to illustrate the controversies Jesus had with the scribes especially but also with the Pharisees and Sadducees. This time the controversies are in Jerusalem rather than in Galilee.

Assessing Albertz' Proposal

Theories of source dependence are inherently conjectural, but Albertz' thesis of two pre-Markan controversy collections is modest and, generally speaking, has much to commend it. It is obvious that scribe

---

Beginnings, 24, 27; Grant, *Earliest Gospel*, 64. Also the contrasting view of W. L. Knox, *op. cit.*, 11 n. 1. Cf., on 2:27-28, Bacon, 31-32; A. E. J. Rawlinson, *St. Mark*, London, 1925, 33; K. L. Schmidt, *Der Rahmen der Geschichte Jesu*, repr., Darmstadt, 1964, 97; Branscomb, 58ff.; also see *infra*, notes 36-40. Nevertheless, even should these verses be secondary, they may have become attached to the collection before Mark appropriated it for his Gospel; this is Albertz' position. Cf. also Taylor, *op. cit.*, 213ff., and the contrasting conclusion of Klostermann, 36. Our own conjecture is that Mark is himself responsible for these two appearances of "Son of man."

[22] Fascher, who is distinctly impressed by Albertz' work here, emends Albertz' proposal at this juncture, as follows: while Albertz holds that the collection had already in essence been formed before these additional passages were inserted, Fascher suggests that the additions became attached only when the individual episodes were *in the process of* being connected. Despite this objection, however, Fascher leaves the general thrust of Albertz' theory of a pre-Markan collection intact (*op. cit.*, 150).

[23] Taylor, however, "with some confidence," contends that Mark himself compiled the collection *before* he wrote his Gospel, and then incorporated his own collection (*op. cit.*, 92); cf. R. H. Stein, "The 'Redaktionsgeschichtliche' Investigation of a Markan Seam (Mc 1:21f.)," *ZNW* 61 (1970), 71 n. 4, where he defines "pre-Markan complexes" as " 'pre-Mark's Gospel' complexes" ("it may very well be that Mark himself was the author of these complexes").

and Pharisee passages in particular are clustered especially in Chapters 2-3 and 11-12: these leadership groups surface unexpectedly for relatively prolonged periods and, then, suddenly vanishing, remain submerged from our vision for chapters at a time. This unevenness, somewhat rupturing the unity of the composition, seems to betray dependence on pre-Markan source material.

The theory of one or two pre-Markan controversy collections has elicited much support from scholars, many of whom have been laudatory of Albertz' work in particular: for example, E. Fascher, B. S. Easton, J. Sundwall, R. Bultmann, V. Taylor, B. H. Branscomb, W. L. Knox, A. J. Hultgren, T. W. Manson, C. H. Dodd, T. A. Burkill and R. H. Stein. [24] Indications that Mark used sources elsewhere in his Gospel increase the likelihood that he used earlier collections here as well. Thus, for example, Easton posits the pre-Markan units of 6:30-7:37 and 8:1-26 on the grounds of their "extraordinary parallelism.... As we cannot believe that Mark was consciously responsible for this long chain of doublets, we must suppose that the two series were circulated separately and that the Evangelist combined them." [25] Branscomb, meanwhile, lists indications which "all constitute positive evidence of documentary sources," and emphasizes, correctly for his day, that "the extent to which Mark rests on these earlier writings has not been sufficiently recognized, due no doubt to the absorption of

---

[24] Fascher, *op. cit.*, esp. 145, 150, 169; Easton, *op. cit.*, 71f., and *especially* "A Primitive Tradition in Mark," *Studies in Early Christianity*, ed. S. J. Case, New York, 1928, 86-87; Sundwall, *Die Zusammensetzung des Markusevangeliums*, Abo, 1934, 14f.; Bultmann, *op. cit.*, 321 n. 2: "...Albertz rightly supposes that Mark knew a collection of conflict stories (I leave open whether in one or two collections)..." (Dibelius disagrees; we do not find his reasoning cogent [*op. cit.*, 219f.]); Taylor, *The Formation of the Gospel Tradition*, 2d ed. repr., London, 1949, 15-17, 87; Branscomb, *op. cit.*, xiiif.: "The series of conflicts between Jesus and the Jewish religious leaders narrated in ii.1-iii.6 evidently came to the editor in written form. *This is generally accepted...*" (italics supplied); W. L. Knox, *op. cit.*, 3 (he is not pleased, however, with the notion of a second collection in Mk. 11-12—see 3, 85ff.); Hultgren, "The Formation of the Sabbath Pericope in Mark 2:23-28," *JBL* 91 (1972), 41; Manson, "Studies in the Gospels and Epistles," in H. K. McArthur, ed., *In Search of the Historical Jesus*, New York, 1969, 26-27; Dodd, "The Framework of the Gospel Narrative," citing also the agreement of K. L. Schmidt that 2:1-3:6 is a pre-Markan unit, in *ibid.*, 112; Burkill, "L'antisémitisme," 16; *idem*, "Strain on the Secret: an Examination of Mark 11:1-13:37," *ZNW* 51 (1960), 31ff.; Stein, "The 'Redaktionsgeschichtlich' Investigation...," 79, and especially the discussion of other pre-Markan complexes as well as Albertz' proposal, 81-82; cf. also T. L. Budesheim, "Jesus and the Disciples in Conflict with Judaism," *ZNW* 62 (1971), 203-205; Donahue, *Are You the Christ?*, 115ff.; Kee, *op. cit.*, 40-41.

[25] *Gospel*, 72.

scholars in recent years with the study of the oral tradition." [26] He proceeds to conclude that

> by far the greater part of the Gospel rests upon documentary sources...
> [and that] the documents which Mark used had come to him through
> the medium of Christian circles in the great sea-coast towns of the
> Hellenistic world. [27]

F. C. Grant identifies the following as possible derivatives of pre-Markan collections:

1. The day in Capernaum.... — 1:21-39
2. The chapter of parables — 4:1-34
3. The call, appointment, and mission of the disciples — 1:16-20; 3:13-19; 6:7-13, etc.
4. The two parallel accounts of journeys about Galilee and in the north — 6:34-7:37 and 8:1-26
5. The great "central section" on "the Way of the Cross," as Bacon called it — 8:27-10:45
6. The journey to Jerusalem — 10:1, 46-52; 11:1-24
7. The "Little Apocalypse" — for which no more appropriate place could be found than just before the passion narrative. [28]

---

[26] *Op. cit.*, xxiii. Besides the Passion story, Branscomb believes "the more certain of these sources" are reflected in Mk. 2:1-3:6, Mk. 13 (with some material inserted by the Evangelist), the "group of parables concerning the Kingdom of God" in Chapter 4, "the names of the Twelve in iii.16ff.," the compact summary of John the Baptist in Chapter 1, and a source containing "information about episodes which took place around the Sea of Galilee."

[27] *Ibid.*, xxv-xxvi.

[28] *Earliest Gospel*, 62; see also Taylor's discussion of Mark's written sources, including those which he believes Mark himself had earlier composed and only now incorporated (*St. Mark*, 90ff.). A major clue to the use of pre-Markan collections is the clustering in Mark of pericopae on a given subject. The key question is whether Mark himself is responsible for the clustering, as part of his redactional process. H. W. Kuhn, *Ältere Sammlungen im Markusevangelium*, Göttingen, 1971, concludes that Mark utilized only four such collections—a highly conservative estimate—one of these consisting of four controversies in Mk. 2:1-12, 15-17, 18-20, 23-24 followed by 27-28. While many scholars agree that 6:30-7:37 and 8:1-26 are a doublet and accordingly reflect the incorporation of pre-Markan collections (e.g., Easton, *Gospel*, 72; Grant, *Earliest Gospel*, 62; Taylor, *St. Mark*, 628; cf. P. J. Achtemeier, "Toward the Isolation of Pre-Markan Miracle Catenae," *JBL* 89 [1970], 265-291; and "The Origin and Function of the Pre-Markan Miracle Catenae," *JBL* 91 [1972], 198-221; Kee, *op. cit.*, 33ff.), Kuhn will not concur. Central to W. H. Kelber's review of Kuhn (*JBL* 93 [1974], 306ff.) is the objection that Kuhn tends to underrate the extent of Mark's use of earlier collection material in some places and to underrate elsewhere the importance of redaction. While Kelber rightly contends that "form criticism and redaction criticism must operate in conjunction," both these methods ultimately depend on what are essentially subjective judgments. As we have indicated, discussion of pre-Markan sources is unavoidably conjectural; regrettably, while we aim for certainty, we must rest content with plausibility.

Despite this favorable assessment, with which we ourselves generally concur, we feel Albertz' conjectures can be challenged in three major respects, this from the standpoint of redaction criticism:

First, Albertz did not realize the extent to which Mark transferred material from both of Albertz' proposed collections to places other than Chapters 2-3 and 11-12. Albertz wrongly assumed that the pre-Markan collections are presented in the Gospel pretty much intact, with Mark playing only a minimal editorial role—that the collections are neatly imbedded in the text, and we can locate them without much difficulty.

Second, Albertz did not recognize that the key to reconstructing the parameters of each pre-Markan controversy collection lies neither with the assigned geographic settings (2:1-3:6 having been set in Galilee; 11:15-12:40 in Jerusalem) nor with the manner in which controversy traditions are clustered (one chain of pericopae in Chapters 2-3, the other in Chapters 11-12) but rather with the way in which Mark has distributed the group *titles* throughout his Gospel. Because Albertz focused on the substance of the controversies but gave the titles of the groups scant attention, he posited collections with the wrong configurations.

Third, Albertz failed to relate the Markan Passion narrative to his analysis of the controversy collections, and he thus did not realize the extent to which Mark's revision and incorporation of the traditions underlying Chapters 14-15 account for the manner in which the titles of Jewish leadership groups are distributed in Chapters 1-13.

Sometimes, only the correct questions will generate correct answers. In our judgment, the correct questions, overlooked by Albertz and later scholars, are these:

1. Why is it that, in spite of the common goal they are alleged to share (the destruction of Jesus), the Jewish leadership elements are unnaturally and artificially grouped into two separate camps of conspirators—chief priests + scribes + elders, on the one hand, and Pharisees + Herodians, on the other—such that
   a. the Pharisees and the scribes (while themselves cooperating with each other on occasion) have no contact whatsoever with each other's allies; and
   b. the chief priests and the elders have no contact whatsoever with the Herodians?
2. Why is it that the Herodians and especially the Pharisees are depicted as so actively harassing Jesus and plotting his destruction in the first unit of Mark, Chapters 1-13, and yet do not even make an appearance in the Passion narrative when these plans are

4

brought to fruition? (Pharisees were present in the Sanhedrin trying Paul [Acts 22:30ff.]; why not in that trying Jesus?)

3. Why is it that the scribes, who appear as subordinates to the chief priests in the Passion narrative, are possessed of a far more impressive stature—akin to that of the Pharisees in authority and interests—in Mk. 12:28-40 (and certain other passages in Mk. 1-13)?

4. Why is it that Pharisees and Herodians, whom Mark seems to associate with Galilee, suddenly emerge in Jerusalem in Mk. 12:13ff.?

5. Why is it that scribes appear so much more frequently in Mark than any other leadership group (and are limited neither to one unit of Mark nor to one geographic area [29])?

We believe these five questions can be answered satisfactorily only on the assumption that Mark relied on three written controversy sources:

a. An early Passion tradition informing him about chief priests, scribes and elders in *Jerusalem*.

b. A collection of pericopae concerning scribes which was either set in *Jerusalem* or assigned by Mark to a Jerusalem setting.

c. A collection of pericopae involving Pharisees and Herodians which was either set in *Galilee* or assigned by Mark to a Galilean setting.

Speaking but generally for the moment, we would resolve the five questions as follows:

Response #1: Pharisees and Herodians were each mentioned in only one of the three Markan sources in question—both in the same source. And this source never mentioned either scribes or chief priests or elders. As for the other two sources, one presented only scribes, the other only chief priests + scribes + elders. This explains why the Jewish leadership elements in Mark seem unnaturally and artificially grouped into two separate camps of conspirators (chief priests + scribes + elders, on the one hand, and Pharisees + Herodians, on the other)— such that neither the Pharisees nor the scribes have contact with each other's allies, nor their allies with each other. [30]

Response #2: The traditions of the Pharisees' and the Herodians' plotting against Jesus are derived from only one of Mark's three sources

---

[29] Pharisees and Herodians are limited to only the first unit, Mk. 1-13; chief priests and elders (and Sadducees) are limited to only one geographic region, Judaea.

[30] The sole departures from this scheme—the juxtaposing of scribes with Pharisees in Mk. 7:1, 5; cf. 2:16—result from Mark's redactional procedures, accommodating his sources to one another; these will be treated in Chapters Four and Five.

(and very likely the latest source). The early Passion tradition knew of chief priests, scribes and elders, but not of Pharisees or Herodians. Possibly, Mark chose not to introduce these two groups into the Passion narrative because the latter was a tightly knit story and the inclusion of Pharisees and Herodians would crowd the stage. This combination of factors might explain why, in the canonical Gospel, neither the Pharisees nor the Herodians appear in the Passion narrative, despite their active participation earlier in plotting Jesus' destruction.

Response #3: Scribes were mentioned in two of Mark's three sources: the early Passion tradition plus a collection of scribe pericopae given a Jerusalem setting. The image of the scribes in the latter was distinctly Pharisaic; but in the former it was indistinct. These considerations explain why scribes appear only as subordinates to the chief priests in the canonical Passion narrative and yet are possessed of a more impressive stature—akin to that of the Pharisees themselves—in Mk. 12:28-40 (and certain other passages in Chapters 1-13).

Response #4: Mark constructed his Gospel in two geographic phases: the early ministry in Galilee; the last week in Jerusalem. The material from the Pharisee/Herodian collection was either set in Galilee or assigned there by Mark. Here these two groups plotted Jesus' death. The early Passion tradition, however, made no mention of these groups. Mark seems to have recognized the anomaly: two groups who plotted to dispose of Jesus were not in Jerusalem for the fulfillment of their plans. While Mark hesitated to introduce them into the Passion narrative (cf. #2, above), he did at least bring them to Jerusalem by severing one pericope from the Galilee collection and transferring it to Jerusalem. That pericope is now placed at 12:13ff. This explains why Pharisees and Herodians, whom Mark always seems to associate with Galilee, suddenly emerge in Jerusalem in this one pericope in Chapter 12.

Response #5: Scribes were the only group which appeared in two of Mark's three sources. That is one reason why scribes are mentioned so much more frequently than any other leadership group in Mark. Another reason is the following: In order effectively to interweave the two units of his Gospel (Chapters 1-13 and 14-16), Mark struggled to move the Passion narrative triad "on stage" as early as possible— but, of the "chief priests, scribes and elders," the scribes were the only group Mark could comfortably depict in a setting outside of Jerusalem. He himself, therefore, frequently interpolated scribes into Chapters 1-13. This also explains why the scribes are the only leadership group to appear not only in both units of Mark but also both inside and outside Judaea.

These, then, will be our adjustments of Albertz' theory. An earlier attempt to revise Albertz' work was undertaken by B. S. Easton, who found Albertz' suggestions "so fruitful" as to inspire his own examination of the problem of the controversy traditions. [31] Easton considerably trimmed down Albertz' two proposed pre-Markan collections and then coalesced them into but *one* of eight pericopae only:

Mk. 2:13-17	The Call of Levi; on Eating with Tax-Collectors and Sinners
2:18-22	On Fasting
2:23-28	On the Sabbath (Gathering Corn)
3:1-6	On the Sabbath (Healing the Man with the Withered Hand)
12:13-17	On Tribute to Caesar
12:18-27	On the Resurrection
12:35-37	On David's Son
12:38-40	A Warning against the Scribes

Easton argued that Mark bisected this collection, assigning the first four pericopae to the Galilean ministry and the second four to Jerusalem.

The strongest point in Easton's analysis is his contention that 12:13-17 is a direct continuation of 3:1-5 or 3:1-6; [32] this observation seems correct, and has been recognized as such by others. [33] The

---

[31] "A Primitive Tradition," 87.

[32] It is unclear, as already noted, whether 3:6 is pre-Markan or Markan editing (cf. *supra*, n. 19). See Easton, 89ff.; later, he states: "Albertz, to be sure, treats (page 5) 3:6 as the original conclusion of 2:1-3:6, which he regards as an independent tradition. But he overlooks the relation between 3:6 and 12:13, as well as the fact that 2:1-12 differs from the other controversies both in contents and form" (93 n. 1; see also *Gospel*, 131).

[33] Verse 13 has been adjusted by Mark so as to conform with its present context. The "they" spoken of is a continuation by Mark from 11:28 and 12:12. In its original form, however, 12:13 followed smoothly after 3:5 (see below). See especially Branscomb, *op. cit.*, xxiii. W. L. Knox, *op. cit.*, 89, also asks whether this pericope (i.e., 12:13ff.) may not have been "transferred by Mark to its present position"; cf. also T. W. Manson, "The Life of Jesus," *BJRL* 28 (1944), 134-135; Burkill, "Anti-Semitism...," 39 n. 2. Both Branscomb and Easton feel the reason for the transfer was Mark's belief that the payment of tribute called for a Judaean setting. Taylor, *St. Mark*, 478, notes: "The reference [in 12:13] to the court party of Herod Antipas is strange in this context and may indicate that the story belongs to the Galilean period." But he adds: "At the same time the reference to the Herodians agrees well with the Lukan tradition that Antipas was present in Jerusalem at the Passover season (Lk. XXIII.7)" (*ibid.* and n. 1). What Taylor apparently fails to

appropriate follow-through, however, is two-fold: 1) to dissociate 12:13-17, 34b from the rest of Chapter 12 instead of positing a single source extending over the eight pericopae; and 2) *to detach 3:6 from 3:1-5 and to append it to 12:13-17, 34b.* [34] We believe that whatever the general scope of the collection underlying parts of Chapters 2 and 3—whether the reconstruction proposed by Albertz (2:1-3:6; we

---

consider is that the Lukan account is an imaginative embellishment of Mk. 12:13, and hardly a confirmation of it! Luke is concerned to demonstrate that all present in Jerusalem perceive Jesus' innocence. Pilate observes this three times (23:4, 14, 22); the centurion perceives this (23:47); and even one of the criminals crucified beside Jesus exclaims "this man has done nothing wrong" (23:41; cf. the parallels in Mark and Matthew). If the Herodians are present in Jerusalem, as Luke undoubtedly inferred from Mk. 12:13, then, quite plausibly, Herod Antipas is present there as well, and himself may be shown as making the observation that Jesus is innocent; and such is the account that Luke indeed fashions. Why else is it that only Luke records such a significant episode (see S. Sandmel, "The Trial of Jesus: Reservations," *Judaism* 20 [1971], 70)? On Luke's possible association of Herod Antipas with Herodians, see *supra*, Chapter Two, n. 17. If Mk. 12:13 can indeed be coalesced with 3:6, it is possible that this "one" verse was the only mention of "Herodians" and that "the leaven of Herod" or "the leaven of the Herodians" in 8:15 was an attempt to bring 8:15 into conformity with 3:6 (see *supra*, Chapter Two, n. 15). It is also possible that 3:6 was originally the *concluding* verse of 12:13ff. and that Mark attached it instead to 3:1-5.

[34] 12:34b ("and after that no one dared ask him any question") makes little sense in its current position; the conversation between Jesus and the scribe (vv. 28-34a) has been amicable. Rather, v. 34b is the logical conclusion of 12:13-17, and refers in turn not only to the "question" in vv. 14-15 but also to the questions or challenges in 2:16, 18, 24 and 3:2. Mark himself has severed v. 34b from 12:17 because, following 12:13-17, Mark wanted the Sadducees and thereafter the scribe to "ask him" questions (vv. 23, 28)—so clearly he could not allow 12:18-27 to be prefaced with the statement: "no one dared ask him"! See Bacon, *Beginnings*, 174; W. L. Knox, *op. cit.*, 87; and especially Cadoux, *op. cit.*, 221; also J. Weiss, *Das älteste Evangelium*, Göttingen, 1903, 272. When Mark severed 12:13-17, 34b from 3:1-5, he either then constructed 3:6, patterning it after 12:13 (this accounting for the resemblance between the two verses), or 3:6 originally came after what is now 12:34b but became juxtaposed to 3:1-5 when Mark transferred the "Tribute" pericope to Chapter 12. The original sequence, in other words, was "Healing the Man with the Withered Hand" (3:1-5), "On Tribute to Caesar" (12:13-17, 34b), "The Plotting Against Jesus" (3:6), with what is now 3:6 originally concluding the Tribute pericope rather than concluding 3:1-5. This solution is attractive because it presents the Herodians in an encounter with Jesus (12:13ff.) *before* they are moved to plot his destruction (3:6); and it shows the Pharisees in cooperation with the Herodians (12:13) *before* they enter into conspiracy with them (3:6). We believe, moreover, that 3:1-5; 12:13-17, 34b; 3:6, in sequence, were the conclusion of a series of confrontations (including at least 2:15ff.; 2:18ff.; and 2:23ff.). How then explain the conspiracy undertaken in 3:6 by the Pharisees and Herodians? It arose not because Jesus gave the "wrong" answer in 12:13ff. but because his answers throughout the whole series were consistently too skilled for his opponents. In exasperation, therefore, "the Pharisees went out, and immediately held counsel with the Herodians against him, how to destroy him" (3:6).

prefer 3:5) or something less extended—verses 12:13-17, 34b (plus 3:6) were originally linked with that source, and Mark himself has detached the Tribute pericope and transferred it to the Jerusalem context so much later in the Gospel.

Despite the importance of the option he proposes, we cannot agree with Easton that only one pre-Markan collection is involved. He does not detect the severing of 12:34b from 12:17 to allow for the inter-positioning of vv. 18-34a, a phenomenon indicating that two different written sources have here been joined and intermeshed. Easton seems correct in associating 12:13-17 with 3:1-5 (or 6) but wrong in as-suming that other pericopae in Chapter 12 (vv. 18-27, 35-37, 38-40) must likewise have been so attached.

Moreover, Easton categorically dismisses 12:28-34 from the col-lection without adequately accounting for its presence in Mark *at this juncture*—or indeed its presence in Mark at all. Why would Mark himself have chosen to insert here a pericope so highly complimentary to scribes, especially one which shows Jesus' favorable attitude toward teachings from the Law of Moses? Nowhere else does Mark say any-thing particularly kind about the scribes or the Law. We can far better account for the presence of the passage here by assuming that Mark found 12:28-34a already connected with 12:18-27; the especially fine linkup of these pericopae in v. 28 could have been the work of a pre-Markan editor. We should not overlook how accurately these verses, including v.28, portray not only what scribes and Sadducees stood for but how they were related to each other. Mark is so often weak in defining leadership groups, and especially in relating them to each other; why do these two pericopae furnish precision in both respects? We believe not only that both passages derive from a source but that they were connected in that source, and that, accordingly, Easton errs in omitting 12:28-34.

If we accept 12:28ff. as a unit connected with 12:18-27, Easton's theory of but one lengthy pre-Markan collection breaks down further. Certain tensions emerge between the first part of his proposed collection and the second part. As we shall show *in subsequent pages*, the first section (including 12:13-17, 34b) dealt *originally* only with Pharisees and Herodians, while the other section (from which 9:11-12a, 13ab has been displaced) dealt with scribes and not with Pharisees at all.

Moreover, the scribes in Easton's proposed collection are strongly Pharisaic in image. Easton accordingly has not accounted for why his *one* proposed pre-Markan source uses two terms—"Pharisees" and "scribes"— for persons who could be construed as being one and the same. We submit that the scribe pericopae have a different provenance, and date earlier, than the Pharisee pericopae. The scribe passages show Jesus and the scribes sharing positive (Pharisaic) sentiments toward certain of the contents of the Law (12:28-34a) and (Pharisaic) sentiments toward resurrection (12:18-28) and (Pharisaic) opposition to the Sadducees (12:18ff.); they also show Jesus' disaffection with the scribes—but *not* over the issue of the Law or its ritual observance (12:35-40; and, as we shall indicate shortly, 9:11ff.). The Pharisee pericopae, on the other hand, depict Jesus and the Pharisees as arch-enemies, split precisely over the issue of observance of the Law. Naturally, scholars may be tempted to infer that the scribes are Pharisaic in doctrinal matters but it is only the Pharisees proper who are pre-occupied with matters of ritual and calendrical observance as specified in the Written and Oral Law. The possibility remains, however, that scribes and Pharisees are different terms for the same societal element, and what we have here is not one but two separate collections focusing on different categories of objection to Jesus but involving the same protagonists, termed in one collection "scribes" and in the other collection "Pharisees."

At this juncture, however, let it suffice simply to say that, despite the three serious shortcomings, Albertz' theory of two pre-Markan collection (underlying, respectively, the controversies in 2:1-3:6 and 11:15-40) is more compelling than Easton's theory of only one collection; nevertheless, Easton and others following him are correct in their perception that 12:13-17 was originally connected with 3:1-5 (or 6) —in fact, the most plausible sequence would be 3:1-5; 12:13-17, 34b; 3:6 [35]—a possibility which Albertz never considered. Whatever the precise delineations of these two separate collections, the seams where Mark wove them together are still visible at 12:17 and 34b.

Redefining the Scope of the Two
Proposed Controversy Collections

As we have seen, scholars confident that Mark used earlier sources for his controversy traditions consider the following configurations reflective of the scope of those sources: 2:1-3:6 and sections within 11:15-12:40. We, just as other scholars, are here operating in the realm

[35] See the end of note 33 and of note 34.

of conjecture, but we question whether these blocks of material which scholars have proposed are really the most plausible.

The pericopae commonly seen as derivative of the first proposed source are:

Mk.	2:1-12	The Paralytic and Forgiveness
	2:13-14	The Call of Levi
	2:15-17	On Eating with Tax-Collectors and Sinners
	2:18-22	On Fasting
	2:23-28	On the Sabbath (Gathering Corn)
	3:1-6	On the Sabbath (Healing the Man with the Withered Hand)

It must be acknowledged that there are primary and secondary strata in a number of these pericopae, and that it is virtually impossible in some cases to determine whether the secondary elements are themselves pre-Markan or added by Mark himself. Accordingly, it is not simply a question of ascertaining which complex of pericopae reflects the scope of the proposed pre-Markan collection but whether certain secondary strata can themselves still be considered part and parcel of the material which Mark received.

Regrettably, it is sometimes even unclear *which* strata should be designated primary and which secondary. Most scholars, for example, consider Mk. 2:23-28 to be composite; yet one must note the divergent analyses in the scholarly literature. One view holds that there are two units here: 2:23-26 and 2:27-28, and that the latter verses are secondary (added either by Mark or a predecessor). [36] Another suggestion, however, is that 2:27-28 is an early saying, with the story of the disciples in the grainfield providing framework for the saying. [37] Still another position considers 2:23-24, 27 as earlier than the other verses, with 2:25-26, 28 "possibly ... added at the time the five conflict stories [2:1-3:6] were collected"; 2:23-24, meanwhile, "was ... attached to 2:27 as a setting for it." [38] Thus, in a pericope of but six verses, there are at least three major scholarly positions as to which are the primary and secondary if not tertiary strata.

---

[36] This view is held by K. L. Schmidt, Albertz, Bultmann, Dibelius, A. E. J. Rawlinson, Taylor, E. Schweizer and A. Suhl; see the bibliographical data in Hultgren, *op. cit.*, 38 n. 1.

[37] See F. W. Beare, "The Sabbath Was Made for Man?" *JBL* 79 (1960), 135, and *The Earliest Records of Jesus*, Nashville, 1962, 92-93.

[38] Hultgren, *op. cit.*, 41.

Moreover, such a determination may carry with it important implications. In our present example, for instance, the ramifications would concern how "Son of man" is to be understood. For if 2:27-28 is one unit, then there arises a need to translate the term "man" in 2:27 and "Son of man" in 2:28 consistently—either as "man" or "Son of man." [39] On the other hand, if vv. 27 and 28 are not a unit, then the verse mentioning "Son of man" is probably later: "The very form of the saying—'hence,' or 'so that'—and its dependence on vs. 27, which is complete without it, suggests that the addition is inferential and editorial." [40]

Even if the separation of strata in the other pericopae of 2:1-3:6 is not as complicated as in the preceding example, the problem remains as to whether the secondary strata are themselves Markan or pre-Markan. Mk. 2:5b-10, for example, is an insertion into the pericope extending from verses 1 to 12. [41] In 2:18, it is possible that "now John's disciples and the Pharisees" is secondary, there being "originally no specification as to who the enquirers were." [42] We have already touched upon the problem of the form-critical breakdown of 3:1-6 [43] and upon those verses in the proposed collection as a whole, 2:1-3:6, which Albertz and Fascher themselves designated as secondary strata, [44] albeit disagreeing on when they were introduced.

---

[39] On the former position, see C. C. Torrey, *The Four Gospels: A New Translation*, 2nd ed., New York, 1947, 73; also L. S. Hay, "The Son of Man in Mark 2.10 and 2.28," *JBL* 89 (1970), 74; on the latter position, cf. T. W. Manson, *Coniectanea neotestamentica* 11 (1947), 145.

[40] Grant, *Earliest Gospel*, 64.

[41] See Bultmann, *op. cit.*, 15 ("vv. 5b-10 ... is clearly constructed for the miracle story, and not originally an independent unit"), 52; also Taylor, *Formation*, 66-68; *St. Mark*, 191-192, 199; Weeden, *op. cit.*, 20 n. 2; Branscomb, *op. cit.*, 45; Bacon, *Beginnings*, 24, 26; W. Bousset, *op. cit.*, 77-78; Klostermann, *op. cit.*, 25; Donahue, *Are You the Christ?*, 82; cf. Kee, *op. cit.*, 35-36. See *infra*, Chapter Four, note 27.

[42] Bultmann, *op. cit.*, 19. "That Mark added the statement is possible, and, so far as the allusion to the Pharisees is concerned, is probable" (Taylor, *St. Mark*, 208). "It would appear that 'the Pharisees' and 'the disciples of the Pharisees' are mentioned because, at a time earlier than the composition of Mark, the story was included in a group of 'Conflict-stories' illustrative of the breach between Jesus and the Rabbis" (*ibid.*, 210). That mention of Pharisees and their disciples may be editorial is suggested by J. Wellhausen, *Das Evangelium Marci*, 2nd ed., Berlin, 1909, 18; Klostermann, *op. cit.*, 31f.; Lohmeyer, *Evangelium*, 59; Rawlinson, *op. cit.*, 30-31 (who feels the fasting was in mourning for John the Baptist, with his disciples being the ones fasting); C. G. Montefiore, *The Synoptic Gospels*, I, London, 1927, 58; Perrin, *Rediscovering*, 79; Olmstead, *op. cit.*, 105.

[43] *Supra*, n. 19.

[44] *Supra*, n. 22.

Our present concern, however, is with the delineation of the *wider* scope of the presumed pre-Markan sources, not with analysis of each pericope on an individual basis. Are the proposed limits, 2:1-3:6, the most plausible estimate of the first collection, as is posited by Albertz and so many others? We propose that the configuration of this collection was significantly different.

We are not at all persuaded that 2:1-14 belongs with the succeeding material. Thematically, 2:1-12 shares nothing in common with what follows. While the controversies in 2:15-3:6 deal mostly with facets of ritual and calendrical observance, and feature in particular the Pharisees, chief authorities on such matters, 2:1-12 is basically a miracle pericope and not a controversy at all; "Albertz ... overlooks ... the fact that 2:1-12 differs from the other controversies both in contents and form." [45] Moreover, as noted already, the *controversy* element within 2:1-12, namely, 2:5b-10, is itself definitely an insertion, possibly by Mark himself. Verses 13-14, meanwhile, deal with the commissioning of Levi as a disciple, and could have been placed here by Mark solely because of an association of Jesus with tax collectors in 2:15f. [46]

While denying that the pre-Markan collection would have contained these pericopae, we find it plausible to suggest that two additional pericopae were included: 7:1ff. as well as 12:13-17, 34b. Though there is disagreement as to how 7:1-23 should be analyzed, [47] we feel that its nucleus originally stood in connection with 2:15-3:6, perhaps even heading this series. Verses 7:1ff. and the other pericopae mentioned all deal with the same general problems of ritual observance, with Jesus and/or his disciples under attack for errant behavior in the eyes of the Pharisees in particular. Generally speaking, each of these pericopae has the same structure—a question or challenge is posed regarding practices of Jesus and/or his disciples (and Jesus dramatically responds to the challenge):

---

[45] Easton, "A Primitive Tradition," 93 n. 1.

[46] While Easton began the collection with 2:13 rather than 2:1 (*ibid.*, 90), T. W. Manson correctly eliminated vv. 13-14 as well as 1-12 ("The Life of Jesus," 135). Bacon, meanwhile, conjectured that 2:1-5a is connected with earlier material, in Chapter 1 (vv. 14-39; see *Beginnings*, 27).

[47] Mk. 7:1-2, 5, 15 represents the essence of the disputation. Bultmann holds the basic section is vv. 1-8; Dibelius and A. Meyer, however, see it as vv. 1-5, 15 (see Bultmann, *op. cit.*, 17). Taylor, meanwhile, sees vv. 5-8 as constituting the "Pronouncement Story on the subject of the tradition of the Elders," with vv. 1-4 "probably the work of the Evangelist" (*Formation*, 82); elsewhere, he identifies the original narrative as "7:1f. + 5-8" (*St. Mark*, 336). See also Kee, *op. cit.*, 210 n. 10.

Mk. 7:1ff.	*Mk. 2:15ff.*	*Mk. 2:18ff.*	*Mk. 2:23ff.*
...And the Pharisees and the scribes asked him, "Why do your disciples not live according to the tradition of the elders, but eat with hands defiled?"	...And the scribes of the Pharisees... said to his disciples, "Why does he eat with tax collectors and sinners?"	...and people came and said to him, "Why do John's disciples and the disciples of the Pharisees fast, but your disciples do not fast?"	...And the Pharisees said to him, "Look, why are they doing what is not lawful on the sabbath?" (followed by 3:1-5, of a slightly different structure)

Significantly, moreover, 7:1ff., in its present context, has no genuine connection either with the material it follows or the material it precedes. These two factors regarding 7:1ff.—its similarity of structure to pericopae in 2:15-3:5, and its lack of firm rootage in its present context—occasion our suspicion that Mark detached this pericope from the pre-Markan collection underlying 2:15-3:6 and transferred it to its present position, perhaps because he felt the discussion of Pharisaic preparation for eating was particularly suitable between the two miracles of feeding in Chapter 6 and 7. [48]

As indicated earlier in this chapter, we espouse the view that 12: 13-17, 34b was initially connected with 3:1-5 or 3:1-6, *and possibly even sandwiched between 3:1-5 and 3:6.* In sum, therefore, we consider the most plausible delineation of the first pre-Markan source to have been, *generally* speaking, not 2:1-3:6 but rather 7:1ff.; 2:15-3:5, 12: 13-17, 34b; 3:6:

Mk. 7:1ff.	On the Washing of Hands
2:15-17	On Eating with Tax-Collectors and Sinners
2:18-22	On Fasting
2:23-28	On the Sabbath (Gathering Corn)
3:1-5	On the Sabbath (Healing the Man with the Withered Hand)
12:13-17, 34b	On Tribute to Caesar (Involving Pharisees + Herodians)

---

[48] In his commentary on 7:1ff., Taylor notes: "Unlike the three preceding stories [i.e., in Chapter 6], there is no link between this narrative and the rest, no temporal or local statement which tells us when and where the incident took place. In form also the narrative is completely different, and for a parallel we have to go back to ii.1-iii.6 and iii.22-6" (*ibid.*, 334). Taylor also suggests that 7:24-37 is a continuation of 6:30-56 (*ibid.*, 96). This requires 7:1-23 to have been an insertion. These observations are entirely compatible with our position that Mark transferred 7:1ff. from a block of Pharisee/Herodian material in what is now Mk. 2:15-3:6. We differ, however, with Taylor's judgment that 2:1-14 and 3:22-26 belong in the same category with 2:15-3:6, but this does not diminish the usefulness of Taylor's observation.

3:6   The Plot to Destroy Jesus (Involving Pharisees +
Herodians). [49]

Our conclusions regarding the second proposed collection resemble
those regarding the first. The scholars who acknowledge an early
collection here have included within their reconstructions pericopae
which bear no integral connection with the collection; moreover, they
have overlooked other material which, in all likelihood, once belonged
to the collection but which Mark has transferred elsewhere.

Mk. 11:15-18   The Cleansing of the Temple
     11:27-33   The Question on Authority
     12:13-17   On Tribute to Caesar
     12:18-27   On the Resurrection
     12:28-34   On the First Commandment
     12:35-37   On David's Son
     12:38-40   A Warning against the Scribes

We have, however, already removed 12:13-17, 34b, and assigned it
to the other pre-Markan collection where we believe it was originally
positioned between 3:5 and 3:6. In addition, with Albertz, we consider
11:18 the result of Markan editing, and, by the same token, we
eliminate 11:27 as well. [50]

Moreover, is there really any basis for connecting 11:15-17 or
11:28-33, on the one hand, with the remaining pericopae proposed by
Albertz? These two episodes reflect *political*-type confrontations introducing and distinctly akin to those in the Passion narrative itself. [51]
Both passages, and especially the first, are employed by Mark to inform
us what grudge the chief priests could have harbored against Jesus—
since up until now they have never encountered him. But the succeeding
passages, 12:18-40, instead discuss theoretical problems of a *doctrinal*

---

[49] Our proposals challenge two of Albertz' arguments but leave two others intact.
If one agrees that the pericopae in 2:1-3:6 are arranged in an order of escalating
tension, as Albertz argued however unpersuasively, then the Evangelist himself is
partially responsible for this; for 2:1-14 did not open the pre-Markan collection but
owes its position to Mark himself. Since 2:10 also, therefore, would not be part of
this pre-Markan collection, Albertz' argument from the premature appearance of
"Son of man" in 2:10, 28 is weakened. His other observations, however—that 1) the
plotting of Jesus' destruction in 3:6 seems premature, and that 2) Mk. 3:22ff.
constitutes an inexplicable letdown in tension—remain important in that they
indicate that 3:6 marks the end of a pre-Markan section which has been introduced
at this juncture in Chapter 2 even though it clashes with Mark's overall literary plan.
[50] On the editorial nature of 11:18, see Albertz, *op. cit.*, 10; Bultmann, *op. cit.*,
36; Dibelius, *op. cit.*, 45; Taylor, *St. Mark*, 461, 464. On 11:27, see Dibelius, 45 n. 1;
Bultmann, 20; Taylor, *Formation*, 65; cf. *St. Mark*, 468; Bacon, *Beginnings*, 164.
[51] Winter, *Trial*, 124-126; see also Donahue, *Are You the Christ?*, 117-118.

and religious nature, primarily in respect to the views of scribes. It is wholly anomalous, therefore, to lump the two pericopae from Chapter 11 with those in Chapter 12.

Accordingly, the original listing of pericopae should be reduced to 12:18-34a, 35-40. [52] At the same time, we suggest the following addition: 9:11-12a, 13ab, [53] which is so evidently similar in form to 12:35-37. [54] We suspect these two pericopae were originally in juxtaposition in this pre-Markan source (though in which sequence cannot be determined) but that, since 9:11-12a, 13ab deals with Elijah, Mark shifted it back from what is now Chapter 12 to just after the story, in Chapter 9, of the Transfiguration—which features an appearance by Elijah. [55] (Similarly, Mark attached 12:41-44 to 12:38-40 because of the mention of "widows" in verse 40. [56])

Precisely as was the case with the other proposed pre-Markan collection, we agree with scholars who posit an early source here but we propose, in *general* terms, a more plausible delineation of the scope of that source—not 11:15-18, 27-33; 12:13-40, but rather 12:18-34a; 9:11-12a, 13ab; 12:35-40:

Mk. 12:18-27	On the Resurrection
12:28-34a	On the First Commandment
9:11-12a, 13ab	On the Coming of Elijah
12:35-37	On David's Son
12:38-40	A Warning against the Scribes

As the other pre-Markan source features primarily the Pharisees, the second pre-Markan source focuses primarily on the scribes. It is significant that scribes, generally speaking, seem randomly distributed throughout the Gospel; yet, in Mark 12, scribe pericopae suddenly

---

[52] These pericopae themselves may, of course, contain elements of Markan editing, such as in the opening of vv. 35, 38.

[53] Mk. 9:12b is secondary. Lohmeyer, *Evangelium des Markus,* 183 n. 1, considers it a gloss. A. Loisy considers it a redactor's insertion (see Grant, *IB,* VII, 778); P. Wernle considers 13c a gloss as well as 12b (see Moffatt, *op. cit.,* 223n). We believe this passage—"and how is it written of the Son of man, that he should suffer many things and be treated with contempt?"—must be considered analogous to the three other editorial predictions of the Passion: 8:31, 9:33; 10:32-34 (cf. W. Wrede, *Das Messiasgeheimnis,* 3rd edition, Göttingen, 1963, 82; Q. Quesnell, *The Mind of Mark,* Rome, 1969, 146 n. 41; C. J. Reedy, "Mk. 8:31-11:10 and the Gospel Ending: A Redaction Study," *CBQ* 34 [1972], 188-197; B. Lindars, *New Testament Apologetic,* London, 1961, 81).

[54] Grant, *Earliest Gospel,* 61.

[55] Cf. Taylor, *St. Mark,* 394. Elijah is also mentioned in 8:27f.

[56] So, e.g., Taylor, *ibid.,* 496.

emerge in a cluster. Nowhere else in Mk. 1-13 do even two scribe pericopae follow one another; here in Chapter 12, however, we have three (and if, as we suspect, 9:11-12a, 13ab was originally juxtaposed to 12:35-37, four). Conceivably, of course, Mark himself was responsible for arranging the pericopae in Chapter 12, but, in such a circumstance, we would have to wonder why he did not string scribe pericopae together elsewhere as well; and if Mark (as opposed to an earlier collector) were himself responsible for the clustering of the scribe pericopae, then would not 9:11-12a, 13ab most likely now appear in Chapter 12? The circumstances seem to have been the opposite: as far as the *controversy pericopae* are concerned, Mark's procedure was to detach a pericope from an original cluster rather than to cluster the pericopae himself (and in this respect his detachment of what is now 9:11-12a, 13ab from the pre-Markan scribe collection would be directly analogous to his detachment of 12:13-17, 34b from the other proposed pre-Markan collection).

Other factors as well point to the existence and incorporation of a pre-Markan source here. Mk. 11:15-18 (the Cleansing of the Temple) and 11:27-33 (the Question on Authority), for example, prepare the reader for the commencement of the Passion narrative. Jesus' having expelled the moneychangers is the last straw for Jewish authorities; the description of this incident, along with the Question on Authority, enables the reader to comprehend how the chief priests, scribes and elders could have become so intent on destroying Jesus by the time we reach 14:1. That which intervenes between 11:33 and 14:1, however—namely, Chapters 12 and 13— is akin neither to what precedes nor to what follows. Nor, strictly speaking, are these two chapters even necessary for the continuation of the narrative line;[57] they actually seem to be interruptions. The pericopae in Chapter 12 are mostly given over to a discussion of theological/doctrinal matters; Chapter 13, meanwhile, stands apart as apocalyptic in nature. Now clearly this does not require that Chapters 12 and 13 must have been pre-Markan units. But Chapter 13, the "Little Apocalypse," did have such a corporate existence prior to Mark's inclusion of it, especially 13:6-8, 14-20, 24-27. *A priori*, therefore, would it be at all surprising if the bulk of Chapter 12 were similarly drawn from a pre-Markan collection dealing with scribes in a Jerusalem setting, which Mark could only incorporate toward the end of the ministry when Jesus, himself involved in the

---

[57] Cf. Winter, *Trial*, 124ff.

controversies, was in the capital? Ordinarily, Mark could have inserted this collection directly before the commencement of the Passion narrative but, since the "Little Apocalypse" was to occupy that slot, Mark had to move the scribe collection one chapter earlier (and, in addition, he severed the Elijah pericope from the collection and transferred it back to Chapter 9 so as to attach it to the Transfiguration scene).

Finally, one cannot help noticing how radically different is the image of "scribes" in Chapter 12 from that in Chapters 14 and 15. In the latter, the portrayal of scribes is nebulous, ill-defined; they have no independence of action—saying nothing on their own, they seem only to follow the lead of the chief priests. As this is true in the Passion narrative, so it is true in the editorial passages based on it: 8:31; 10:33-34; 11:18; 11:27. But in our proposed scribe collection, underlying most of Chapter 12, the identity and societal role of the scribes are far more sharply defined. Consistently within this unit, they loom up as major authorities in their own right; and their opposition to the Sadducees is in strange contrast to the scribes' subservience, in the Passion narrative, to the (Saducean?) chief priests.

Noteworthy, also, is the distinctly *Pharisaic* flavor of the scribes in our proposed collection. On the basis of the Passion narrative and its related passages alone, scribes could be construed as Saducean; [58] but in Chapter 12 they are definitely on the Pharisaic side of the ledger both in their rejoinder on resurrection and in the prominence accorded them in the synagogue, a Pharisaic institution, not to mention in their specification of teachings most important in the Pharisaic/rabbinic tradition. Thus, all the scribe pericopae in our proposed collection present a consistent image which contrasts with the image of the scribes in the Passion narrative. Are we to assume that these two widely varying images of the scribes issue from Mark himself, or are they instead the result of Mark's reliance on differing sources for his information? Surely the latter explanation is by far the more compelling.

---

[58] See Chapter Four, notes 41-42, and our discussion of the problem of Saducean scribes in Chapter Five. We ourselves deny that "scribes" in the Passion narrative must necessarily be considered Saducean. Our concern at this juncture, however, is simply to indicate that the indistinct image of scribes in the Passion narrative is different from their clearly Pharisaic image in Chapter 12, and that material in Mk. 12 must, therefore, have had a different provenance from material in the Passion narrative.

CHAPTER FOUR

THE INFLUENCE OF A PRE-MARKAN PASSION TRADITION ON MARK'S TREATMENT OF JEWISH LEADERSHIP GROUPS

The two proposed pre-Markan controversy collections both fall entirely within Chapters 1-13. But we believe Mark arranged Chapters 1-13 in the light of his early Passion tradition. Accordingly, it is vital that the controversy collections be studied in connection with the Passion tradition. The failure of scholars to follow this procedure explains many of the shortcomings in earlier studies of the Jewish authorities in Mark.

Jewish Leadership Groups
in the Pre-Markan Passion Tradition

The Passion narrative in Mark is widely understood as an expansion of an underlying written source. [1] An account of Jesus' last days was presumably already available to Mark even before he composed Chapters 1-13. His Gospel, therefore, is a "passion story with an extended introduction," [2] "written in A.D. 70 or soon afterwards by a person who composed the first thirteen chapters to provide what might be termed a propaedeutic to a suitably adapted form of the traditional passion narrative." [3] Mark's task was to fashion these opening chapters in such a way that they would dovetail perfectly with his predetermined conclusion. Accordingly, the contents and sequence of some episodes in Chapters 1-13 reflect literary needs rather than historical realities:

> It is of crucial importance... that we should recognize *the nature of the purpose behind evangelical presentations of the order of various events* in Jesus' life. *The setting forth of earlier stages of this life*

---

[1] See especially Dibelius, *op. cit.*, 23; Bultmann, *op. cit.*, 262ff., 277-279; Grant, *Earliest Gospel*, 77ff., 175; Taylor, *Formation*, 44-62, and *St. Mark*, 653-664; W. R. Wilson, *The Execution of Jesus*, New York, 1970, 29-30; Sloyan, *op. cit.*, 37-38, 43-44 (esp. notes 11-12); Burkill, *New Light*, 221ff., 229ff.

[2] M. Kähler, *The So-Called Historical Jesus and the Historic Biblical Christ*, trans. C. E. Braaten, Philadelphia, 1964, 80.

[3] Burkill, *New Light*, 264; also 221, and "St. Mark's Philosophy of the Passion," *NovT* 2 (1958), 245-271, on 245; cf. also Winter, *Trial*, 113ff.; W. Marxsen, *Der Evangelist Markus*, Göttingen, 1956, 17; Grant, *Earliest Gospel*, 70-71. See additional listings in Donahue, "Introduction...," in Kelber, 8ff., and especially notes 29 and 63.

was controlled by the notion of them as phases in the development of a literary plan which finds its culmination in the crucifixion. The end was there before the beginning had been thought of.... Traditional elements of the story concerning "earlier events" are so arranged as to supply the reader with a reasonable explanation of the Passion.... Hence no historical or biographical information can be gleaned from the order of the items used concerning the chronological sequence of events in the life of Jesus. [4]

If we accept the theory of a pre-Markan Passion narrative, clearly the responsibility for Jesus' capture and execution was assigned by that source to three Jewish authority groups: chief priests + scribes + elders. In prefacing other chapters to the Passion story, therefore, it would have been incumbent upon Mark to prepare his readers for the predetermined *dénouement*; that is to say, the Passion narrative triad —chief priests + scribes + elders—had to make an appearance in Chapters 1-13. Only if the reader could trace the escalation of their hostility toward Jesus *prior to* 14:1 could their actions against him be rendered sufficiently intelligible.

Scholars accepting the theory of a pre-Markan narrative are certain that this source actually mentioned these leadership groups. Mark himself did not introduce them along with his other revisions of that source. M. Dibelius, R. Bultmann and G. Sloyan are three scholars whose analyses [5] strip Mark 14-15 down to its barest minimum so as to isolate the antecedent core. While their full reconstructions vary considerably from one another, they yet concur that at least the following verses must be pre-Markan: Mk. 14:1-2 represents the opening of the original narrative; 14:43 and 15:1, 3-5, 15b are also primary; so also 15:21, 26, 34, 37. By stringing together the first eight verses, we find the following:

Mk. 14:1-2   It was now two days before the Passover and the feast of Unleavened Bread. And *the chief priests and the scribes* were seeking how to arrest him by stealth, and kill him; for they said, "Not during the feast, lest there be a tumult of the people."

14:43   And immediately, while he was still speaking, Judas came, one of the twelve, and with him a crowd with swords and clubs, from *the chief priests and the scribes and the elders.*

---

[4] Winter, *Trial*, 111; italics Winter's.
[5] Dibelius, *op. cit.*, 178ff.; Bultmann, *op. cit.*, 262ff.; Sloyan, *op. cit.*, 43 n. 11.

> 15:1, And as soon as it was morning *the chief priests, with the*
> 3-5,   *elders and scribes,* and the whole council held a consulta-
> 15b   tion; and they bound Jesus and led him away and
>   delivered him to Pilate.... And *the chief priests* accused
>   him of many things. And Pilate ... asked him, "Have
>   you no answer to make? See how many charges they
>   bring against you." But Jesus made no ... answer, so that
>   Pilate wondered.... And having scourged Jesus, he deliv-
>   ered him to be crucified.

This exercise indicates that, as best we can determine, "chief priests,"
"scribes" and "elders" were present among the Passion traditions Mark
received. [6] The passages in which they appear are integral to the very
structure of the plot. To relinquish them is to relinquish as well the
whole notion of a pre-Markan Passion source which, despite a number
of recent treatments, [7] we are not prepared to do. [8] In our own

---

[6] See also Taylor, *St. Mark,* 653ff.; Winter, *Trial,* 125f.; Burkill, *New Light,* 221, 229.

[7] See P. J. Achtemeier, *op. cit.,* 82ff.; Donahue, "Introduction...," in Kelber, 1-2, 8ff., and the conclusion by Kelber, 153ff.; also E. Linnemann, *Studien zur Passions-geschichte,* Göttingen, 1970; H. C. Kee, *Jesus in History,* New York, 1970, 274; E. Güttgemanns, *Offene Fragen zur Formgeschichte des Evangeliums,* Munich, 1970, 227-229.

[8] We fully agree that "Markan editorial work is as surely evident in this part of his Gospel as in earlier parts" (Achtemeier, *op. cit.,* 83) but this hardly precludes Mark's use of an early Passion source. He exercised his editorial creativity by reworking and considerably enlarging this document. In presenting our own conception of this source (see the following note), we indicate how much of Mark 14-15 must yet be left to Mark's own activity, including especially the trial scene in the Sanhedrin, the story of Peter's denial and related passages disparaging of the disciples, the pericope which aligns the Last Supper chronologically with the Passover Seder (14:12-16), the incident of the anointment (14:3-9), and others. To be sure, some of the accretions to the earliest narrative *may* yet have been pre-Markan (e.g., the story of the naked young man, the institution of the Lord's Supper, the application of imagery from Psalms 22 and 69, the Barabbas episode); but in no way do we deny or even underestimate the degree of Mark's own involvement in the shaping of the canonical Passion narrative. Nevertheless, to dismiss altogether the notion of *a pre-Markan Passion story introducing Mark to the chief priests + scribes + elders* strikes us as totally unwarranted; a redaction criticism which attributes everything to redaction is surely excessive. Many arguments advanced in recent studies really establish very little in disproving Mark's use of an early Passion source: that the Passion story now reflects Mark's theological concerns indicates that he recast his source in conformity with those concerns, not that there was no such source; that "there is no indication ... from the way in which Matthew and Luke make use of the Markan passion narrative that they were aware of a generally accepted, pre-Markan formulation of those events" (Achtemeier, 83) only implies that Matthew and Luke knew no such source, not that Mark himself never knew or used one; that John's agreements with Mark can be explained by John's acquaintance with Mark rather than with a Markan source (see Donahue, in Kelber, 9) indicates nothing about Mark's

reconstruction of the earliest stratum, moreover, we include also Mk. 14:10 (which happens to mention chief priests) and 14:53 (which happens to mention chief priests, elders and scribes). [9]

We further contend that this early narrative was the *only* source which furnished Mark with his knowledge of chief priests, scribes and elders and that *all passages in Mk. 1-13 conjoining chief priests and scribes, or chief priests and scribes and elders, are redactional retrojections by Mark* based on what he himself has learned from the Passion tradition he has received. Such passages are the following:

Mk. 8:31   And he began to teach them that the Son of man must suffer many things, and be rejected by *the elders and the chief priests and the scribes*, and be killed, and after three days rise again.

10:32ff.   ...He began to tell them what was to happen to him, saying, "Behold, we are going up to Jerusalem; and the Son of man will be delivered to *the chief priests and the scribes*, and they will condemn him to death, and deliver him to the Gentiles; and they will mock him, and spit upon him, and scourge him, and kill him; and after three days he will rise."

---

own use or non-use of such a source. To deny outright the existence of a pre-Markan Passion narrative would be rash indeed. Even after marshalling his evidence, e.g., Donahue himself is appropriately hesitant: "The very discovery of a complex tradition history behind the Markan Passion Narrative casts *some* [?] doubt on the validity of postulating an independent and coherent Passion Narrative prior to Mark. The hypothesis of a pre-Markan connected narrative, if not completely abandoned, is *somewhat* [?] shaken" (italics ours). Clearly the existence of the early source cannot be disproved, and we maintain our assumption that it did exist even as we accept Donahue's conclusions regarding the interpolated units and late revisions introduced by the redactor. See Raymond Brown's review of the Kelber volume, *CBQ* 39 (1977), 283-285, reading in part: "The book is clearly intended to overthrow the theory of a pre-Marcan passion narrative, although there is no detailed refutation of Taylor's evidence for Lucan dependence on a non-Marcan passion, and although the non-Marcan elements in John are too easily attributed to Johannine theology" (284).

[9] Our primary concern is simply to indicate that, whatever the scope of this early Passion source—whether a lengthy narrative complete in and of itself, or simply a limited and isolated tradition—this was the source where Mark gained his information about "chief priests + scribes + elders." Since, as just stated, we maintain a belief in a pre-Markan Passion narrative, we now suggest that its earliest stratum underlies the following canonical passages: 14:1-2, 10-11, 17-20, 26, 32, 35-36 (minus the translation of "Abba"), 43-46, 53; 15:1, 3-5 (minus "again" in v.4 and "further" in v.5), 15b, 21-22 (minus the translation of Golgotha), 25-27, 34 (minus translation), 37. With regard to the canonical passages which we have left out as secondary, some represent material which Mark himself has inserted; others, while secondary to the original stratum, are yet pre-Markan. Even passages which are pre-Markan may now contain Markan vocabulary as a result of Mark's editorial activity.

| 11:18 | And *the chief priests and the scribes* heard it and sought a way to destroy him; for they feared him, because all the multitude was astonished at his teaching. |
| 11:27 | ...And as he was walking in the temple, *the chief priests and the scribes and the elders* came to him.... |

Of these three groups, the one best comprehended by Mark must have been the chief priests. Even someone relatively unfamiliar with the Holy Land—as we believe was the case with Mark—could apprehend the role of "chief priests" in Judaean society. Writing, probably in Rome, during or after the Great Rebellion (66-73), Mark would surely have heard of the institution of the Temple; certainly, the triumphal procession of Jewish captives through the streets of Rome in 71 heightened the vividness of the Temple establishment for residents of that city, as did, later, the sculptured contours on the Arch of Titus which depicted the scene: triumphant legionaries bearing the Temple spoils—including the Menorah, the altar of the shewbread, and the silver trumpets. [10]

Whether or not Mark wrote from Rome in particular, it is likely that anyone reading his Gospel would have understood whom "chief priests" designated. Mark himself was probably partial to the identification of Jesus' enemies in the early Passion tradition as the priestly corps since, during the Jewish revolt in the late 60's, the Temple had become popularly regarded as the geographic and spiritual core of resistance to Roman armies. Roman readers could easily associate the hated Temple establishment of Mark's own time with that Temple group which, according to the early Passion tradition, had orchestrated Jesus' arrest and execution:

> Nothing was more necessary in a Roman milieu than that the responsibility for Jesus' death be removed from the State. How might this be effected? To place the sequence of events within the light of the then important fact of the Jewish revolt in Jerusalem, it was quite clear that the Temple group was one with whom no sympathy would be wasted either by Roman or Christian. Whether or not the author of the earliest Gospel saw the triumphal procession along the Sacred Way, many of his readers saw it, and to them it would have seemed but just that the group whose resistance to Rome might be most readily personified should be pictured as the group responsible for the death of the Lord of the cult. To those who were the original

[10] The Arch of Titus was erected after the death of Titus in 81; see Brandon, *Zealots*, 143 n. 2; 225 n. 1. Brandon's discussion of "the interest stirred among Roman Christians by the spoils of the Temple" merits attention (227-230).

readers of this work the "scribes, chief priests, and elders" would be sufficiently comprehensive. [11]

Sharing as they did a common enemy, [12] namely, the Jewish leaders, Christianity and Rome could naturally construe themselves as allied.

As for the other two Jewish leadership groups furnished Mark by this early Passion tradition—scribes and elders—it is uncertain what these groups meant to Mark initially. Whether he comprehended them or not, however, Mark had to come to terms with them. For the early Passion tradition had informed him that these two groups, in conjunction with the chief priests, had played an active role in disposing of Jesus. Was the reader to encounter them for the first time only in (what is now) 14:1? Clearly, Mark was obliged to detail how their hostility toward Jesus had escalated from its very inception. Only so could the reader satisfactorily account for Jesus' fate at their hands.

Yet how *had* that hostility arisen? Could Mark himself have known? While the early Passion tradition may have been a self-contained unit, even a full narrative, in terms of Mark's needs it commenced only *in medias res*—it intimated nothing concerning any prefatory developments. Clearly, Mark had two options: search for other background sources on Jesus' enemies; or improvise. He chose both. He had at his disposal two collections about Jesus in relation to Jewish leadership groups, one source focusing on Jewish authorities called "scribes," setting them in Jerusalem, the other mentioning two groups called "Pharisees" (with whom Mark may have had some personal acquaintance) and "Herodians." *In neither of these two collections were*

---

[11] Riddle, *op. cit.*, 103.

[12] Of course, such an inference would be hardly accurate in that the Temple authorities were generally the great bastion of Roman support in Judaea. In Jesus' day, the High Priest and his colleagues were likely Rome's henchmen, not opponents, High Priests generally being appointees of the Procurator (*Antiq.* XVIII. ii.2 [xviii. 29-35]). In the succeeding decades as well, Sadducean elements could be expected to support a maintenance of the *status quo* from which they benefited. Rather it had been the so-called fanatical groups, among whom Josephus, himself in Rome, was soon to list "Fourth Philosophers" and "Zealots," who prosecuted the war with greatest vigor and were in the main responsible for prolonging the resistance. But it is doubtful whether such subtle distinctions were manifest either to Mark or his audience, for whom the simple fact was that, in the late sixties, the Temple in Jerusalem (never mind exactly who or why) was symbolic of and at times the actual center of resistance to Rome, and only with its destruction was rebellion utterly crushed. That Jesus was believed to have predicted the destruction (cf. Mk. 13) and that it could be construed as punishment of the Jews rendered this reasoning all the more compelling.

chief priests or elders mentioned. Mark incorporated both these collections, apportioning them as suited his needs, and then improvised extensively in accommodating them to one another, and both of them to his early Passion tradition.

Mark's Redactional Procedures

Certain problems inevitably impose themselves on any author beginning a composition whose ending is already predetermined. Material to be incorporated into the earlier sections of the work (in our case, Mk. 1-13) must continually be reshaped and redirected so it will dovetail perfectly with all dimensions of the preconceived conclusion (in our case, the Passion tradition which Mark received).

One of Mark's tasks in Chapters 1-13, accordingly, was to assist his readers in understanding why the chief priests, scribes and elders in that conclusion had come to hate Jesus sufficiently to wish his execution. This would have been a relatively simple procedure if only these groups as a triad had appeared in traditions which Mark was to incorporate into Chapters 1-13. But there is no indication that Mark had any such traditions at his disposal.

While he did have three sources for Jewish leadership groups, they did not dovetail well at all. The original Passion tradition (and indeed the full canonical Passion narrative as well!) limited Jesus' enemies to chief priests, scribes and elders, but never mentioned the additional groups of Pharisees or Herodians. Meanwhile, the Pharisee/Herodian source (corresponding roughly to 7:1ff.; 2:15-3:5; 12:13-17, 34b; 3:6) never mentioned the triad appearing in the Passion narrative and, as we shall attempt to demonstrate shortly, even the mentions of "scribes" in 2:16; 7:1, 5 were not original to this source. The scribe source (corresponding roughly to 12:18-34a; 9:11-12a, 13ab; 12:35-40), moreover, never mentioned chief priests or elders or Pharisees or Herodians, and the very image of the scribes in this source varied so significantly from their portrayal in the Passion tradition that the two sources hardly complemented each other. Considerable skill would thus be required if Mark were to accommodate these sources to one another smoothly.

Mark's task would have been far more manageable if he had only better understood who each leadership group had been. This would have given him more leeway to exercise his patterns of creativity so evident in other dimensions of his Gospel. He may have personally encountered Pharisees in the Dispersion, [13] and most likely he could have inferred who was indicated by the title "chief priests"; nevertheless, as we contended in Chapter Two, Mark's "Herodians" and "elders," and also "scribes" (in the Passion narrative) seem so ill-defined as to occasion our doubts as to how much he truly knew about them. And so unclear was Mark concerning how scribes and Pharisees are to be distinguished from one another that Matthew, depending upon him, seems to be left completely bewildered.

How, then, did Mark manage to incorporate his two controversy sources and accommodate them both to one another and also to the original Passion tradition? The following is our reconstruction.

Since Jesus' arrest, condemnation and execution in Jerusalem represented the climax of his ministry, Mark determined not to permit Jesus to appear in the capital on any previous occasion. An artificial geographical dichotomy thus developed, as he was planning his Gospel, between a conclusion affixed to Jerusalem and earlier developments rooted elsewhere, primarily in Galilee where Jesus had lived and extensively taught.

Naturally, provision had to be made in the Gospel's structure for a transitional period (Chapters 10-13), bridging the ministry in Galilee (Chapters 1-9) with the Passion Week in Jerusalem (Chapters 14-16).

---

[13] How early the Pharisees were present in the Diaspora is difficult to estimate. Paul describes himself as having been a Pharisee (Phil. 3:5). And his training in Pharisaism was not acquired in Palestine, let alone Jerusalem; Acts 22:3 is tendentious (cf. references in Chapter One, n. 21; also our article, "Judaism, Hellenistic," *IDB* Suppl. Vol., 508-509). To be sure, however, we cannot be certain precisely how to evaluate Paul's statement that he was a Pharisee nor do we know much about Pharisaism in the Greek Dispersion (see Sandmel, *Genius of Paul*, 13-15, 44ff.). E. Rivkin's short reconstruction of Pharisaism's spread into the Dispersion is very probably correct (Prolegomenon to *Judaism and Christianity*, ed. by W. O. E. Oesterley, H. Loewe and E. I. J. Rosenthal, repr., New York, 1969, lv ff.); we lack confidence, however, as to precisely how early such developments occurred. H. Mantel's documentation of the activity of Pharisaic emissaries in the Dispersion is useful (*Studies in the History of the Sanhedrin*, Cambridge, Mass., 1961, 190ff.), but reliance on rabbinic literature cannot confirm Pharisaism's widespread presence in the Dispersion much before 70; on the other hand, there is much about the pre-70 period to which rabbinic literature fails to attest. It is likely that Pharisees emigrated in significant numbers during the reign of Alexander Jannaeus who persecuted them in the early first century B.C.E. At any rate, of all the Markan Jewish leadership groups, it is the Pharisees who were the most familiar—and possibly the only group familiar—to Mark in the Dispersion around 70 C.E. How familiar is another question; if 7:3-4 is Mark's own interpolation, he hardly manifests a well-rounded understanding of the Pharisees' platform.

These transitional chapters would serve to recount not only Jesus' journey from Galilee to Judaea and his entry into Jerusalem, but also those specific catalytic developments transpiring in the capital itself which eventuated, in 14:1ff., in the activation by the Jerusalem triad of their plot to arrest Jesus. Surely it would simply not do for the major villains of the piece—the chief priests + the scribes + the elders—to make their first appearance in the plot as late as 14:1, already virtually the close of the drama, without any hint supplied concerning the origin and escalation of their animosity toward Jesus.

It is hardly surprising, therefore, that Jesus is made to encounter these very groups—naturally all three appearing as a unit—soon after he has entered Jerusalem. Not only are the two mentions of these groups—11:18 and 11:27—both editorial, but they should be perceived as representing but two instances in Mark's overarching scheme to retroject the three conspiratorial groups from Chapters 14-15 into Chapters 1-13. Verse 18 is particularly important for it effectively alerts the reader as to why the chief priests, who are to assume the leading role in the Passion narrative, become upset with Jesus, for heretofore no indication has been given as to how Jesus has in any way trespassed on priestly prerogatives or interests.

On the other hand, a retrojection only as far back as Chapter 11 would hardly have been satisfying. For it would still appear as if the Jerusalem conspirators embarked on stage only the last moment— during Jesus' final week—and this could occasion the inference that Jesus had been caught unawares by groups whom he had previously neither known nor even anticipated. In such a circumstance, his fore-knowledge called into question, Jesus could easily be construed victim rather than victor. Optimally, therefore, these three conspirators should have been introduced in controversy with Jesus far earlier in the Gospel. But for Mark to have moved them back even into Chapter 9 would have been exceedingly problematic; for Jesus, at that juncture, was not yet in Judaea let alone Jerusalem, and what could Mark legitimately portray chief priests, scribes and elders doing roaming outside their home base let alone in the distant Galilean countryside?! Surely, in Mark's conception, the chief priests were particularly immobile, tied as he presumed they were to the Jerusalem Temple. As for the elders, how could Mark (or we ourselves, for that matter), on the basis of the Passion tradition he received, really have surmised who "elders" actually were or how they functioned in society? Even in the canonical Passion narrative, when do the elders make a single independent appearance let alone do or say a single thing distinctive? To present elders any earlier than Chapter 14, Mark would have been constrained to team them up at least with the chief priests, since this was the only manner in which they ever made an appearance in the Passion story.

Two options did remain, however, and Mark availed himself of both. In the first place, while he could not "bodily" introduce the chief priests or elders into Galilee, he could easily forewarn the reader as to their existence and ascribe to Jesus, while *he* was in Galilee, an awareness of their identity and a foreknowledge of what they would do to him once he entered Jerusalem. And on several occasions this is precisely what Mark does: 8:31, in Caesarea Philippi; 10:33-34, in rural Judaea; and less explicitly in 9:30-32, in Galilee, and also 9:12b. All these reflect Mark's "penchant for preparing the reader for what follows." [14] Again, many scholars have granted that these passages are editorial, but have not discerned their kinship with other passages mentioning chief priests + scribes + elders (or only chief priests + scribes) in Chapters 1-13, all of them editorial work by Mark himself in his endeavor to move the Passion narrative personnel on stage as early in his drama as possible.

More importantly, Mark still had at his disposal one group from among the Jerusalem triad whom he could indeed "bodily" retroject into Galilee—the "scribes." They impressed Mark as more mobile than the chief priests and more distinctive than the elders—because Mark knew about them from a special collection of scribe pericopae, a pre-Markan collection which Albertz, Easton and so many others have suspected underlies pericopae in Chapters 11-12, but which we have more precisely delineated as underlying 12:18-34a; 9:11-12a, 13ab; 12:35-40. While the pre-Markan Passion tradition was the sole source for Mark's knowledge of "chief priests + scribes + elders" as a *triad*, the scribe source instructed Mark about "scribes" in particular—and Mark undoubtedly assumed that these scribes were identical

14 Donahue, *Are You the Christ?*, 206-207. On the three predictions of the Passion, see Bultmann, *op. cit.*, 25; Dibelius, *op. cit.*, 225; both consider them editorial. So also Grant, *Earliest Gospel*, 66 ("these are clearly secondary, and are now generally recognized as such"), and 179 n. 5 (the Gospel "grew backwards from the passion narrative"; "the three passion announcements are indubitably by Mark himself, and secondary, that is, no part of the early tradition"); Klostermann, *op. cit.*, 119; Schmidt, *op. cit.*, 218; Taylor, *St. Mark*, 124, 377-378; G. Strecker, "Die Leidens- und Auferstehungsvoraussagen im Markusevangelium," *ZTK* 64 (1967), 16ff.; C. J. Reedy, *art. cit.*, 188-197; Burkill, *New Light*, 218ff. On the editorial nature of 9:12b, see *supra*, Chapter Three, n. 53.

with the scribes mentioned but never adequately described in his pre-Markan Passion material. Since Mark already knew of Jerusalem "scribes" from that early Passion tradition, this second source on scribes was easily accommodated with the Passion narrative itself, and indeed would have been juxtaposed directly before it had not the so-called "Little Apocalypse" intervened to displace it.

The chief virtue of this special scribe source was not simply that it furnished Mark with several interesting episodes for inclusion in his Gospel but that it supplied him with sufficient information about the scribes so he could confidently and comfortably interpolate scribes into the earliest chapters of his Gospel—precisely what he could not manage to accomplish with either chief priests or elders. The scribe source afforded Mark material to work with, clues as to the scribes' position as teachers and authoritative interpreters in society at large and in the synagogue in particular, [15] clues as to the scribes' ideological concerns especially regarding Jesus' messianic credentials. [16] This meant that Mark was now equipped with sufficiently distinct data about the scribes to retroject and interject them into selected pericopae even during Jesus' Galilean mission, wherein they could be available to join with those challenging Jesus' credentials [17] and serve as a foil for Jesus in the eyes of the populace, especially in a synagogue setting. [18] For needless to say, Mark was now at liberty to have the scribes appear in rural synagogues—his special source had clearly opened that option for him; [19] while the chief priests and the elders were restricted to the Temple environs in Jerusalem, the scribes had free access to any synagogue even in the Galilean countryside!

And thus it is that, in order to have Jesus encounter at least one of the Jerusalem conspiratorial triad early in the Gospel, and thereby render the Passion narrative the fully anticipated culmination of Mark's lengthy introduction (Chapters 1-13), Mark portrayed scribes in Galilee, *where none of his sources located them*! But having taken such license, Mark carefully specified that these scribes had, after all, "come down from Jerusalem." Scholars who conjure up a variety of excuses for scribes to have undertaken such excursions into Galilee have over-

---

[15] Mk. 12:28-34a, 38-40.
[16] Mk. 9:11-12a, 13ab; 12:35-37.
[17] E.g., Mk. 2:6f.; 3:22.
[18] E.g., Mk. 1:21f.
[19] Mk. 12:39.

looked the point altogether: the *sole* reason why they had "come down from Jerusalem" is that Mark himself had brought them! [20]

Let us approach the matter more systematically by examining every passage in Mk. 1-13 mentioning chief priests or scribes or elders. If our hypothesis is correct, there should be grounds for viewing as editorial every mention of chief priests or elders and every mention of scribes outside, of course, the pre-Markan scribe source—each such mention being the result of Mark's having shifted his Jerusalem-based personnel back into earlier scenes of the drama, so as to knit together the two distinct units of his composition (Chapters 1-13 and 14-16), and to sow the seeds of hostility between Jesus and his Passion narrative enemies as early as feasible in that first unit.

There are only four passages in Mk. 1-13 which mention either chief priests or elders or both (8:31; 10:33-34; 11:18; 11:27), and in the case of all four we have already indicated the grounds for considering them editorial (along with two additional passages, 9:30-32 and 9:12b, which, while not explicitly mentioning Jewish leadership groups, are nevertheless related to those passages which do).

There are sixteen passages mentioning scribes in Mk. 1-13. Five (9:11; 12:28, 32, 35, 38) were derived from the pre-Markan scribe collection (12:18-34a; 9:11-12a, 13ab; 12:35-40), as we have already argued in detail. Are the remaining eleven passages editorial? Four are the same editorial verses as those mentioning the chief priests + the elders, or only the chief priests. There thus remain to be considered only the following seven passages in which scribes appear or are mentioned:

---

[20] Branscomb is typical of scholars accepting Mark at face value, reconstructing history based on Mark's editorial adjustments: "In spite of the fact that Galilee was under a different political power, religious matters would have been directed by the council of scribes which met in the 'Hall of Hewn Stones' on the temple mount, 'whence the law went out to all Israel.' Whether these scribes were a committee sent by some official authority, or a voluntary group who were interested in the work of this Galilean prophet, is not said.... The movement of repentance which he [i.e., Jesus] endeavoured to create was national in scope, and it is not surprising that we find references to scribes from Jerusalem who were sufficiently interested to attend upon His teaching" (*op. cit.*, 69-70). Countless other scholars as well have not realized that it was not the scribes who were interested in "attending upon" Jesus; it was *Mark* who was interested in the scribes' attending upon Jesus! So also do many scholars struggle to define the scribes in their relation to the Pharisees, all the while never questioning whether the Markan testimony that there was a relation between two such *separate* (?) groups is historically reliable! See also Moffatt, *op. cit.*, 222n.

Mk. 1:22   And they were astonished at his teaching, for he taught them as one who had authority, and not as *the scribes*.

2:6   Now some of *the scribes* were sitting there, questioning in their hearts....

2:16   And *the scribes* of [*or* and] the Pharisees, when they saw that he was eating with sinners and tax collectors, said to his disciples, "Why does he eat with tax collectors and sinners?"

3:22   And *the scribes* who came down from Jerusalem said, "He is possessed by Beelzebul, and by the prince of demons he casts out the demons."

7:1   Now when the Pharisees gathered together to him, with some of *the scribes*, who had come from Jerusalem....

7:5   And the Pharisees and *the scribes* asked him, "Why do your disciples not live according to the tradition of the elders, but eat with hands defiled?"

9:14   And when they came to the disciples, they saw a great crowd about them, and *scribes* arguing with them.

We submit that all seven of these mentions of scribes are editorial. Mk. 1:22 is evidently secondary, [21] as is the clause mentioning scribes in 3:22. [22] In fact, the very specification in 3:22 that the scribes "came down from Jerusalem" in itself arouses our suspicions as to the editor's personal involvement. [23] The identical circumstance underlies the ap-

---

[21] Bultmann, *op. cit.*, 209; Weeden, *op. cit.*, 20, n. 2; 22 n. 7. When one omits v.22 from 1:21-27, neither the verse itself nor its mention of scribes is in any way missed. The contents of v.22 seem to us modeled on those of v.27, with "and not as the scribes" tacked on; the motifs of astonishment, teaching, authority are all present in v.27. And if v.27 is secondary, then v.22 all the more so (cf. Bultmann, 209 n. 2; Dibelius, *op. cit.*, 237). Bultmann, believing that the motif of "teaching" is secondary to that of "healing" in this pericope, suggests the omission of "a new teaching! With authority" from v.27, and hence all of v.22 along with it. "The passage so emended exhibits the typical characteristics of a miracle story, and especially of an exorcism..." (209-210). Dibelius observes, though in a different connection, that here "Jesus is described as teaching, but we ... learn nothing about His teaching..." (237). In any event, Mark is responsible for the passage mentioning scribes in 1:22.

[22] Mk. 3:22ff. has been spliced here into another pericope; 3:22, the passage mentioning scribes, therefore has no connection with 3:21, the latter being picked up again in 3:31. See Bultmann, *op. cit.*, 13, 29; Taylor, *St. Mark*, 237; Branscomb, *op. cit.*, 69; Bacon, *Beginnings*, 37; cf. W. L. Knox, *op. cit.*, 32; Dibelius, *op. cit.*, 46-47. The end of v.22 is a doublet; the beginning of the verse, "And the scribes who came down from Jerusalem," is, according to Bultmann, "the only piece of Marcan editing" (13; see also Weeden, *op. cit.*, 20 n. 2), but it is the only piece we are concerned to indicate is editing.

[23] Note Dibelius' correct perception: "It is very possible that the passage [3:23-26] already lay before the evangelist in this form. He must then have biographically evaluated the occasion, which was handed down without the circumstances, *and made the scribes come from Jerusalem*..." (*op. cit.*, 220; italics ours).

pearance of scribes in 7:1 [24] (and, naturally, in 7:5 along with it); the clause in 7:1, "with some of the scribes, who had come from Jerusalem," is an attempt by Mark to introduce scribes into what is basically only a Pharisee passage—originally attached to the rest of the pre-Markan Pharisee/Herodian complex (2:15-3:5; 12:13-17, 34b; 3:6) but detached by Mark and transferred to Chapter 7. [25] Meanwhile, the appearance of scribes in 9:14 (if not the verse as a whole) is surely editorial. [26]

Only two "scribe" passages remain to be considered: 2:6 and 2:16. The former falls within a larger interpolated unit, as we have already indicated; we feel the interpolation, 2:5b-10, is by Mark himself. [27] Thus far, then, out of our sixteen mentions of scribes in Mk. 1-13, we believe five are from the pre-Markan scribe source, and another ten are redactional.

This leaves us only with 2:16. While variants of this verse are of interest—is the text "the scribes *of* the Pharisees" or "the scribes *and* the Pharisees"? [28]—the passage should be viewed in the light of our

---

[24] See especially Riddle, *op. cit.*, 111; Bultmann, *op. cit.*, 52 ("Scribes and Pharisees are always present when the editor needs them ... as typical participants in debate.... In Mk. 7:2 [*sic*] the *grammateis* were summoned from Jerusalem!"); Weeden, *op. cit.*, 20 n. 2.

[25] See *supra*, Chapter Three, note 48. Alternatively, though less likely, 7:1f. could as a whole be editorial, having been based on what was learned from 7:5. If this is the case, we conjecture that v.5, coming from the pre-Markan Pharisee/Herodian source, did not mention scribes; Mark inserted scribes and then formulated an introductory statement (v.1) mentioning both groups. We prefer the other option, however, that v.1 (without the scribes) is from the pre-Markan collection; Mark himself then introduced scribes from Jerusalem, and then had to mention both groups again in v.5 to pick up after the parenthetical interruption (vv.3-4). "The Pharisees and the scribes" in v.5 "looks very much like a repetition of the parallel passage in 1, caused by the insertion of the parenthesis 3f. If so, the original narrative is 1f. + 5-8" (Taylor, *St. Mark*, 336). So also Bacon, *Beginnings*, 86. In either event, however, the presence of scribes is redactional.

[26] The scribes are "forced" into this passage, "pressed in only as a belated addition; they have no business there at all..." (Bultmann, *op. cit.*, 52). So also Weeden, *op. cit.*, 20 n. 2, who considers a number of references to the masses as redactional, 9:14-15 among them (22 n. 7). Taylor agrees that the presence of "scribes" here is editorial along with the introductory passage as a whole, i.e., vv.14f. It is also to be noted that "in the rest of the story they are not mentioned and there is no reference to a dispute with them" (*St. Mark,* 396-397).

[27] See above, Chapter Three, n. 41. Interestingly, this is the only passage accusing Jesus of blasphemy, aside from the trial scene, Mk. 14:55-65 (also probably a Markan interpolation).

[28] On the problem, see Chapter Three, n. 3. The *lectio difficilior* would be "scribes of the Pharisees." Many manuscripts, as expected, would correct it to "scribes and Pharisees," because this is the simpler reading. On the other hand, it is unclear why

overall hypothesis. For thus far *every* mention of a group from the Jerusalem triad in Chapters 1-13 (outside of the special scribe source) has appeared to be redactional—all four mentions of chief priests (plus two related passages, 9:30-32; 9:12b), both mentions of elders, and ten mentions of scribes. Can we thus seriously doubt that here also in 2:16 Mark has inserted scribes? Whether the adjoining word which Mark also inserted was "of" or "and" is beside the point. The significant factor is that "scribes" may not have been in the pre-Markan passage. Consider as well that the pericope in question is part of that pre-Markan complex featuring the Pharisees and Herodians. Scribes have been inserted into one other pericope from that collection, in 7:1, 5; we should be cautious in considering "scribes" in 2:16 original in a controversy collection consistently featuring Pharisees instead— indeed, the presence of scribes here has been characterized as peculiar. [29]

The strongest confirmation of our position is the following: 2:16 and 7:1, 5 are the sole exceptions to the otherwise rigid compartmentalization of the two conspiratorial camps throughout the Gospel—chief priests + scribes + elders, on the one hand, and Pharisees + Herodians, on the other. If throughout the Gospel, in the more than fifty mentions of Jewish conspiratorial groups (twenty-one mentions of scribes, fourteen of chief priests, eleven of Pharisees, five of elders, and two or three of Herodians), no member of one camp ever encounters or is juxtaposed to a member of the other camp except in these three instances, 2:16; 7:1, 5, and if the presence of scribes with Pharisees in 7:1, 5 is so transparently editorial, then how are we to evaluate the mention of "scribes" in juxtaposition to "Pharisees" in 2:16 unless we attribute it to Mark himself precisely as we have attributed to him "scribes" in 1:22; 2:6; 3:22; 7:1, 5; and 9:14? In the pre-Markan collection, therefore, it was not the "scribes of the Pharisees" or the "scribes and the Pharisees" who protested against Jesus' eating with tax collectors and sinners; it was only the Pharisees. It was not the Pharisees "with some of the scribes, who had come from Jerusalem," who com-

---

the more difficult reading arose in the first place. There is nothing analogous to it in Mark, and we view Acts 23:9 as deriving from it rather than confirming its accuracy. See further discussion in Chapter Five.

   [29] W. L. Knox, however, fails to understand why "Bultmann ... regards it as ridiculous that 'the scribes from Jerusalem come simply to see the disciples eat'" (14, citing Bultmann, *Die Geschichte der synoptischen Tradition*, 2d ed., Göttingen, 1931, 16). Burkill terms their presence "historically unlikely" ("Anti-Semitism in St. Mark's Gospel," 39 n. 3).

plained that Jesus' disciples ate with unwashed hands; in the pre-
Markan pericope, it was only the Pharisees who so complained. [30]

As we shall explain in more detail shortly, gone is the need to
assume, on the basis of Mark, that the scribes were the intellectual elite
of the Pharisees or indeed that scribes and Pharisees must be separate
groups whose relationship to each other should be defined, for in
reality the scribes and Pharisees never appeared *together* in any one of
Mark's sources: his two sources for scribes (the Passion tradition he
received and the pre-Markan scribe collection) never mentioned Pharisees, and his source for Pharisees (the pre-Markan Pharisee/Herodian
collection) never mentioned scribes. Since it was Mark who brought
the scribes and Pharisees of his separate sources together, the possibility
even remains that the terms "scribes" and "Pharisees" refer to one and
the same societal element, but that Mark, unfamiliar with who scribes
had been, failed to detect the synonymity of the usage, and therefore
presents us with two groups rather than one. Because, however, he has
left their respective allies just as unrelated to each other as were the
separate sources from which he lifted them, we have the scheme of
rigid compartmentalization of the two conspiratorial camps: the Pharisees associating only with the Herodians, and the scribes only with the
chief priests and the elders.

Assessing the Analysis by P. Winter

Our analysis has focused not on the contents of the controversy
traditions *per se* but rather on Mark's mentions *by title* of the five
Jewish leadership groups specifically said to have conspired against
Jesus. While many scholars have agreed that sources underlie the
controversy traditions, the titles of the groups have not been utilized
as the clue to delineating the scope of each source. For that matter,
we have also investigated mentions of the group titles in pericopae
falling outside the proposed collections and have contended that appearances of chief priests + scribes + elders, or chief priests + scribes
alone, outside the Passion narrative (i.e., in Chapters 1-13) and appearances of scribes alone in Chapters 1-13 (but of course in pericopae
outside the proposed scribe source) are editorial. Quite possibly the
same is true of mentions of Pharisees outside the proposed Pharisee/

---

[30] Our argument, in both these instances, is only that Mark introduced "scribes"
into a pericope which mentioned only Pharisees initially. But in the pre-Markan
history of that pericope, "Pharisees" itself could have been an insertion or substitution.
Cf. Dibelius, *op. cit.*, 64.

Herodian source. Our theory also well accounts for the otherwise puzzling absence of Pharisees from the Passion narrative.

There is at least one other scholar on Mark who has placed his primary focus not on the controversy traditions *per se* but rather on the appearance and distribution of the group *titles*, and this is P. Winter. Because his analysis is both excellent in some respects and yet seriously deficient in others, it attracts our extended attention.

Winter believes that the criterion of group names can be used to separate strata of Mark in terms of their respective chronology. He notes that in the introductory chapters of Mark the enemies of Jesus do not include the chief priests or elders, while *"the oldest synoptic tradition* [Chapters 14-15] (however restyled it may have become in the process of literary formulation) *does not include the Pharisees among the enemies of Jesus at all."* [31] We must thus recognize two categories of hostility: 1) hostility towards Jesus ascribed to the chief priests and their associates; 2) hostility towards Jesus ascribed to the Pharisees.

> The two categories belong to entirely different situations and come from periods in the history of the early Church that are divided from each other by several decades. The traditional cycle in which "the chief priests" function as the adversaries of Jesus is of relatively early origin; various traditions depicting "the Pharisees" engaged in a campaign of opposing Jesus belong to a much later date. [32]

Winter's further reasoning lends itself to presentation in tabular chronological form:

Passages mentioning
    chief priests + scribes (+ elders) . . .   "correspond to the earliest stratum of tradition"

Passages mentioning
    only scribes . . . .   correspond to a later stratum

Passages mentioning
    Pharisees . . . .   correspond to a still later stratum [33]

---

[31] *Op. cit.,* 124; italics Winter's.

[32] *Ibid.*

[33] To quote Winter exactly: "Those passages in Mark in which the chief priests *and* the elders and scribes appear as Jesus' foes correspond to the earliest stratum of tradition, earlier than those in which 'the scribes' appear alone. Such passages again are of earlier origin than any passage mentioning the Pharisees..." (125, italics Winter's).

Since "there is *no traditional link* between the narratives incorporated into Mark in which hostility towards Jesus is ascribed to *the chief priests* and their associates, and those narratives in which *the Pharisees* are assigned an antagonistic role," and since "these quite distinct segments of tradition were first connected by the Evangelist," [34] Mark's presentation of Jewish leadership groups should not inspire any historian's confidence.

Winter's analysis also helps account for the absence of the Pharisees from the Passion narrative despite their prominence in the "earlier" chapters and also for the absence of the chief priests and the elders before the Passion narrative, "except for isolated references in Mk. 11."

> The principal conclusion to be drawn ... is that the controversy stories of which most of chapters 2, 3 and 12 consists have not the same background, and do not bespeak the same situation or the same *milieu*, as the report of Jesus' arrest in Mark 14 and of his execution in Mark 15. [35]

On the basis of our own analysis, however, the strata in Mark should be distinguished somewhat differently than Winter assumes:

I. Passages mentioning chief priests + scribes (+ elders) *from the Passion narrative only.* [36]

II. Passages, mentioning only scribes, which are *from the pre-Markan scribe collection* (corresponding roughly to Mk. 12:18-34a; 9:11-12a, 13ab; 12:35-40).

III. Passages mentioning Pharisees (+ Herodians), which are *from the pre-Markan Pharisee/Herodian collection* (corresponding roughly to Mk. 7:1ff.; 2:15-3:5; 12:13-17, 34b; 3:6).

IV. *All* other mentions of chief priests, scribes or elders, and *all* other mentions of Pharisees, in Mk. 1-13.

The first category of passages, wherein chief priests and scribes (and sometimes elders) are conjoined, comes from the pre-Markan Passion tradition.

Passages incorporated from the pre-Markan scribe collection (the second category) reflect a later concern by the church to gather material on Jesus' relations with this group who, for all intents and purposes, may have been equivalent to Pharisees but under an earlier name. Noteworthy in these passages is the absence of any dissension over

---

[34] *Ibid.*, 124 (italics Winter's).

[35] *Ibid.* (italics Winter's).

[36] Mk. 15:31, however, while possibly still pre-Markan, is found in a secondary stratum of the Passion narrative; see above, n. 9.

the validity of the Law; in one pericope there is even agreement on the subject of important commandments. Dissension over the Law arose only after Paul's teachings became influential. Still, the issues under discussion here—resurrection, Elijah's coming, the ancestry of the Messiah, etc.—while reflecting some of the earliest concerns of the (Palestinian?) church in disputation with Jewish critics, post-date Jesus' ministry as well as the formulations of the earliest Passion traditions.

Passages from the pre-Markan Pharisee/Herodian collection (the third category) are later still, reflecting in their denigration of the Law and the interpreters thereof the period when Pauline teachings had become influential in a Gentile-Christian context.

Finally, all other mentions of chief priests, scribes or elders in Mk. 1-13 are still later, being products of Mark's own redactional activity; and it is probable that isolated references to Pharisees, not included in our reconstructed Pharisee/Herodian source, are likewise redactional. 37

We thus differ from the position of Winter in four respects:

First, Winter does not detect that mentions of chief priests + scribes (+ elders) in 11:18 and 11:27 are Mark's own additions; instead Winter believes that the contents of Mk. 11:15-18, 27-28 were associated with the contents of 14:1ff. before Mark wrote, and that Mark inserted Chapters 12 and 13, which he himself had put together.

Second, Winter believes that passages mentioning scribes alone are later than those mentioning chief priests + scribes (+ elders). But this is true only occasionally. We agree that certain "scribes only" passages —those derived from the scribe source (12:18-34a; 9:11-12a, 13ab;

---

37 Others, e.g., have suspected that "Pharisees" are interpolated into the text in 10:2; see Burkill, *New Light*, 223 n. 57; Bultmann, *op. cit.*, 52; Riddle, *op. cit.*, 11, 115; Taylor, *St. Mark*, 417 (calling attention to views of Wellhausen and Burkitt); also Winter, *op. cit.*, 206; Bacon, *Beginnings*, 138; cf. J. Bowker, *Jesus and the Pharisees*, Cambridge, 1973, 38. The other mentions of Pharisees are in 8:11, 15. It is difficult to assess this section. 8:1-26 is apparently parallel to 6:34-7:37, and the place occupied by the Pharisees in the later sequence, i.e., the brief section in 8:11ff., corresponds to the much longer section in the earlier sequence, i.e., 7:1-23 (Grant, *IB*, VII, 758), with 8:15 belonging with 8:11ff. (*ibid.*, 761). It is wise to heed Bultmann's warning: "There is an active tendency seeking always *to present the opponents of Jesus as Scribes and Pharisees.*... They are always present when the editor needs them ... as typical participants in debate.... It should be clear that in all this the specific statements are the secondary ones.... Naturally I do not mean to banish Scribes and Pharisees from all controversy dialogues; I only want to indicate a tendency of the Tradition, and to issue a warning about the schematic understanding so characteristic of the gospels" (52-54; italics Bultmann's).

12:35-40)—possibly post-date the earliest stratum of the Passion narrative which presents us with chief priests + scribes + elders. Yet
these same scribe passages antedate those passages in *Mk. 1-13* which
mention chief priests + scribes (+ elders): 8:31; 10:33-34; 11:18;
11:27; the scribe source is pre-Markan, but these other passages stem
from Mark himself. Moreover, Winter does not distinguish between
"scribes only" passages issuing from the pre-Markan collection and
mentions of "scribes only" for which Mark himself is responsible: e.g.,
1:22; 2:6; 3:22; 9:14; he implies that all passages mentioning scribes
alone derive from the same stratum, but this is hardly correct. Moreover,
mentions of scribes for which Mark himself is responsible are not later
than mentions of chief priests + scribes + elders for which Mark is
responsible—they derive from the same level, that of redaction.

Third, while Winter correctly assigns Pharisee passages to a late
stratum, he does not differentiate between Pharisee passages emanating
from a pre-Markan collection (7:1ff.; 2:15-3:5; 12:13-17, 34b; 3:6)
and mentions of Pharisees which are redactional only. Moreover, there
are certain passages—2:16 and 7:1, 5—which mention scribes along
with Pharisees. Winter has not considered whether Mark himself has
inserted scribes in these passages.

Fourth, and perhaps most important, Winter's zeal to exculpate
the Pharisees from charges of uncharitableness lodged against them has
influenced his analysis. We agree with some of his allegations: that
the Pharisee passages do not derive from early strata in Mark [we
assign them to Stratum III]; that Matthew and Luke have, on occasion,
introduced "Pharisees" into Markan pericopae not mentioning them,
these insertions being almost always pejorative; that traditions of controversy between Jesus and the Pharisees are retrojections of tensions
developing decades later than Jesus' ministry. But the absence of
"Pharisees" from the Passion narrative does not prove, as Winter
presumes, that Pharisees played no role in Jesus' arrest, trial or condemnation for "scribes" in that Passion narrative could have been
Pharisees. Winter refuses, however, to associate these scribes with
Pharisees—to do so would be to admit that Pharisees could indeed
have been conspirators against Jesus (assuming, that is, that the earliest
stratum of the Passion tradition [which mentions "scribes"] is necessarily any the more reliable to the historian than the later strata).

There are four major scholarly positions on defining the scribes in
Mark. Two of these have strongly associated the scribes with Pharisees:
one holds that "scribes" are identical with "Pharisees," the terms either

being synonymous or one term, "scribes," being an earlier means of reference to a group later known by another title, "Pharisees"; [38] the second and predominant view is that "scribes" are the leadership element or intellectual elite of the Pharisaic movement, to be distinguished from Pharisees even though closely associated with them—a position often taking its cue from Mk. 2:16 and 7:1, 5 (N.B.: the very verses into which we contend Mark has interpolated scribes!) in conjunction with Acts 23:9. [39] A third view, however, holds that not all scribes were necessarily Pharisaic since Sadducees also had scribes; accordingly, while some Markan references are to Pharisaic scribes, others could be to Sadducean scribes. [40] Scribes presumed Pharisaic would be those mentioned in 1:22; 2:6, 16; 3:22; 7:1, 5; 9:11, 14; 12:28, 32, 35, 38; scribes would be Sadducean in 8:31; 10:33; 11:18, 27; 14:1, 43, 53; 15:1, 31. [41] A fourth position holds that, even where scribes in Mark seem Pharisaic, in the original edition of Mark they were Sadducean. [42]

Winter divorces himself from each of these positions, including especially the second, the most popular:

> It is one of the commonest fallacies in New Testament exegesis to identify "scribes" with Pharisees. A scribe ... is an "official"; in modern parlance we would use the title "civil servant".... Among the scribes were persons of other than Pharisaic persuasion. The erroneous identification is largely due to the author of the First Gospel [i.e., Matthew] who ostensibly used the terms as synonyms. The First Evangelist, himself a Pharisee by education, developed a pet aversion for that Jewish group from which he had come. [43]

---

[38] See discussion in R. A. Marcus, "The Pharisees in the Light of Modern Scholarship," *JR* 32 (1952), 155; G. F. Moore, *Judaism*, I, Cambridge, Mass., 1946, 43; and especially E. Rivkin, "Defining the Pharisees: the Tannaitic Sources," *HUCA* 40-41 (1969-1970), 205-249; cf. Bowker, *op. cit.*, 1ff.

[39] Note the rendering in Klostermann, *op. cit.*, 28. See Bacon, *Beginnings*, 22; Moore, *op. cit.*, I, 57, 66; Branscomb, *op. cit.*, 50; Taylor, *St. Mark*, 209; Jeremias, *op. cit.*, 246, 258-259; Klausner, *op. cit.*, 288; Finkelstein, *The Pharisees*, 3d ed., I, Philadelphia, 1962, 280.

[40] On the theory that Sadducees had scribes, see E. Schürer, *Geschichte des jüdischen Volkes*, II, Leipzig, 1901-1911, 380ff., 457; ET II.1, 319f., II.2, 11; E. Meyer, *Ursprung und Anfänge des Christentums*, II, Berlin, 1921-1923, 286ff.; Moore, "The Rise of Normative Judaism," *HTR* 17 (1924), 350f.

[41] See discussions in Klausner, *op. cit.*, 122, 320, 334-335; D. Chwolson, *Das letzte Passamahl Christi und der Tag seines Todes*, 2d ed., Leipzig, 1908, 112ff.; Bowker, *op. cit.*, 41.

[42] See Chwolson, *op. cit.*, 112ff.; A. Büchler, *Die Priester und der Cultus im letzten Jahrzehnt des Jerusalemischen Tempels*, Vienna, 1895, 80-87; Olmstead, *op. cit.*, 178ff.

[43] Winter, 209-210, note 25.

Winter's argument is far from compelling. In the pre-Markan scribe source, scribes are definitely Pharisaic, as we have already indicated. [44] The Passion narrative, meanwhile, does not afford us enough information to formulate any definition of scribes at all, not even Winter's designation of them as civil servants; the term "scribes" could *here* be a simple construct, much like "elders," "Herodians," "chief priests." On the other hand, why should we dissociate scribes in the Passion narrative from scribes as we know them from the pre-Markan scribe source? Surely Mark assumed they were one and the same, and here is an instance where Mark may have been correct. Nor can we accept Winter's facile designation of Matthew as the root of the problem. Matthew's confusion of scribes with Pharisees is occasioned by Mark himself and in particular by Mark's interpolation of "scribes" into 2:16 and 7:1, 5. [45]

But despite our divergences from Winter's analysis, we consider his treatment of the Jewish leadership groups the finest we have encountered because his focus is on the distribution of the titles of the groups and therefore he is able to contribute insights lacking in other studies.

Mark's Redactional Problems in Incorporating the Pharisee/Herodian Source

Did Mark really need the *third* stratum of passages, as we have numbered them—that is to say, could he have completed his Gospel satisfactorily without ever mentioning the Pharisees or the Herodians? Most assuredly, he could have omitted them entirely for the leadership groups mentioned in the pre-Markan Passion tradition—chief priests + scribes + elders—were sufficient to carry the whole plot. If all Pharisee/Herodian passages were now deleted from Mark, new readers, when initiated to the Gospel, would sense no inadequacy in the composition.

---

[44] *Supra*, end of Chapter Three.

[45] Moreover, there is no evidence whatsoever that Matthew had been a Pharisee. Legalistic emphases in Matthew need not be construed as reflecting Pharisaic upbringing, nor should legalism and Pharisaism be construed as synonyms (cf. our article, "Judaism, Early Rabbinic," *IDB* Suppl. Vol., 499-505). That Matthew was biased against Pharisaism, however, is clear. What is unclear is whether Pharisees as such were still in existence in Matthew's time and community. In other words, is Matthew responding to Pharisees actually in his community, or only to a Christian recollection of Pharisaic disputations of the past which Matthew now intensifies in his treatment of the controversy traditions?

Undoubtedly, however, Mark was eager to incorporate this material into his Gospel since the controversies in the Pharisee/Herodian collection were highly relevant to Dispersion Gentile-Christian communities. For therein could Jesus be construed as justifying the departures by later Christians from Jewish dietary laws, ritual prohibitions and calendrical observances, areas of concern to Gentile-Christians because of the repeated harassment they underwent at the hands of those whom they perceived as carping Jewish critics. [46]

Jesus' enemies on these matters were not, according to this source, the chief priests, scribes and elders, but rather persons called Pharisees and Herodians. This circumstance was problematic for Mark: the Pharisees and Herodians who here opposed Jesus and were, at one point, said to have actually plotted his destruction were yet never mentioned in Mark's early Passion traditions. Burkill comments: "the suggestion is that the hierarchs and the scribes take up what the Pharisees and the Herodians were the first to plan." [47] We believe, however, that this was not Mark's intention *ab initio*; rather, he was pressed into this artificial scheme. The take-over of the Pharisaic-Herodian plot by the chief priests, scribes and elders is simply the result of Mark's attempt to harmonize two different sources: his early Passion tradition and the Pharisee/Herodian collection.

This Pharisee/Herodian material was thus a mixed blessing. On the one hand, it provided Mark not only with further details as to how and why hostility had developed against Jesus, but also with model responses, paradigms which Mark's own fellow Gentile-Christians might emulate when subjected to criticism by the Pharisees/rabbis of their own day. On the other hand, because Jesus' enemies in these controversies were Pharisees and Herodians rather than chief priests, scribes and elders, Mark could incorporate these traditions only at the price of introducing some discordance and discontinuity into his Gospel!

Mark associated the Pharisees and Herodians with Galilee, though it is unclear whether his source provided this setting or whether it was Mark's own assignment. In either case, however, the association was agreeable to him. For not realizing that "Pharisees" were closely related

---

[46] Bacon's *Is Mark a Roman Gospel?* and Riddle's *Jesus and the Pharisees* remain important reconstructions of this situation. Also useful is D. R. A. Hare's *The Theme of Jewish Persecution of Christians in the Gospel According to Matthew*, Cambridge, 1967; we believe he accepts Acts too uncritically and does not consider that much of what he hypothesizes for Palestine is equally if not more appropriate for a Dispersion context.

[47] *New Light*, 219 n. 49; cf. 218ff.

to, if not synonymous with, "scribes," [48] Mark assumed that Pharisees were not involved in Jesus' arrest in *Jerusalem*, since the Passion narrative omitted any mention of them there; that they were instead based in Galilee was, accordingly, acceptable, especially since the Pharisees' allies, the Herodians, were probably associated by Mark with Galilee. It is likely that, rightly or wrongly, he connected them with Herod Antipas, whom he mistakenly regarded as "king" of Galilee; [49] hence, Mark was content to locate Herodians there along with Herod. [50] The term "Herodians" is not his, but rather that of his source, [51] so whether or not the Herodians existed in Mark's own day is not necessarily pertinent.

Accordingly, to establish continuity in his Gospel, Mark had to smooth the transition between, on the one hand, Jesus' encounters in Galilee with the Pharisees and Herodians and, on the other hand, Jesus' downfall in Jerusalem at the hands of the chief priests, scribes and elders. Mark's major effort in this regard was to detach what we know as Mk. 12:13-17, 34b from the Pharisee/Herodian collection (which we have conjectured corresponded roughly with 7:1ff.; 2:15-3:5; 12:13-17, 34b; 3:6); thereby he brought Pharisees and Herodians into Jerusalem just before the arrest and trial of Jesus. There, these too could participate, along with the Sadducees and scribes, in engaging Jesus in conversation and argumentation prior to the arrest engineered by the chief priests, scribes and elders.

So as to cushion our surprise at the presence of Pharisees in Jerusalem, Mark opens his transitional chapters by having the Pharisees encounter Jesus just as he crosses into Judaea—this passage being editorial. [52] Meanwhile, by specifically inserting scribes into the Pharisee/Herodian collection, in Mk. 2:16 and 7:1, 5, Mark created a makeshift partnership between the Pharisees and one of the groups appearing in the Passion narrative Mark received, such that the Pharisees have at least vicarious participation in effectuating the events ending the Passion Week.

---

[48] See Rivkin, *art. cit.*, other references, *supra*, n. 39, and further discussion, *infra*, end of Chapter Five.

[49] Mk. 6:14. Luke may have made the same association; see *supra*, Chapter Two, n. 17.

[50] The variant readings of 8:15 ("Herod" or "Herodians") do not of course actually demonstrate that Mark associated Herodians with Galilee but do indicate how easily such an inference could be made.

[51] In the pre-Markan development of this source, however, it is of course conceivable that Herodians is secondary (cf. *supra*, n. 30).

[52] See *supra*, n. 37.

The absence of the Pharisees from the Passion narrative does not mean we should accord them no role in Jesus' condemnation and execution. If "scribes" refers to persons later termed "Pharisees," the Pharisees were indeed present in that account, at least implicitly. Of course, however, we cannot know how reliable even the early Passion traditions really are or whether even the chief priests, scribes or elders were actually involved in the events which are now irretrievably beyond our grasp.

CHAPTER FIVE

IMPLICATIONS FOR THE HISTORIAN

In examining the Jewish leaders in Mark, we have presented a series of problems we feel scholars have not addressed and a single idea we feel resolves them all. Often, however, there inheres in source, form and redaction critical studies an element of conjecture, and this is true in our analysis as well. We are satisfied that our thesis is correct, but in our view there is insufficient evidence either fully to verify or fully to invalidate our proposals. Our aim, therefore, has been simply to present a plausible case. We will now summarize our position before indicating possibly significant implications of our study for the historian.

Summary

Our basic concerns have been to determine how familiar Mark was with the Jewish leadership groups of Jesus' time, where he received his knowledge about them, and how he used this information in constructing the framework of his narrative line. Essentially, we have been dealing with three chronological levels of Markan material: the latest level that of redaction, preceded by the level of written or oral sources, with the earliest level that of historical reality.

On *the level of redaction*, we have confronted in Mark a situation different in a major respect from what we encounter in the later Synoptists. We actually possess one of Matthew's and Luke's prime sources, Mark himself. Accordingly, where Matthew and Luke alter Mark, especially in ways diverse from one another, we have the potential for isolating those characteristic procedures and theological nuances which betray, respectively, the hands of these two Evangelists themselves. [1] We remain in a far less advantageous position with Mark, however, because we possess none of his sources.

Yet it is on *the level of sources* that we have especially focused in this study. Rightly, scholars must beware the circularity which can so easily assume control in source criticism, wherein the very pre-

---

[1] See discussion in Achtemeier, *op. cit.*, 15f.; Donahue, "Introduction: From Passion Traditions to Passion Narrative," 15ff.

sumption of sources inevitably generates conclusions "confirming" their existence and then defining their scope and content. But with regard to the controversy traditions, we find the case for sources more than merely plausible. In addition to citing arguments of scholars similarly disposed, we have advanced our own: Certain peculiarities in Mark's treatment of the Jewish leaders *require* an assumption of three-source dependency. Only thus can we explain the artificial compartmentalization of the five Jewish conspiratorial groups into two separate camps—chief priests + scribes + elders, on the one hand, and Pharisees + Herodians, on the other—and also explain the departures from this pattern in 7:1, 5 (cf. 2:16); only thus can we also resolve three ancillary problems—the absence of Pharisees from the Passion narrative, Mark's unusually frequent mention of scribes, and the presence in Mark of two radically contrasting images of scribes.

As we have shown, one factor has been particularly helpful in defining the scope of the three proposed sources: the pattern of distribution of the group titles in Mark. Other linguistic criteria cannot be as usefully applied because the sources Mark incorporated are not preserved to us still in their original formulation. Present in many of the pericopae in question are various editorial touches by Mark, alterations and interpolated material unrelated to the original traditions. Some scholars presume similar contributions by pre-Markan editors of these sources. [2] Accordingly, while we find the assumption of the three sources indispensable, the delineations we have proposed—7:1ff; 2:15-3:5; 12:13-17, 34b; 3:6 and 12:18-34a; 9:11-12a, 13ab; 12:35-40 plus a pre-Markan Passion tradition [3]—are rather loose in the case of most pericopae. Realistically, this has been our only choice. Without an independent means of verification, any attempt at word-by-word restoration of all the pericopae of each source would be only fanciful; it would also widen the purview of our presentation well beyond our original intention which was simply to explain the peculiarities we have noted in Mark's treatment of the leadership groups.

Implications of Our Study for the Historian

Obstacles Confronting the Historian

We have focused primarily on the two latest levels of Markan material, "redaction" preceded by "sources"; yet what can be known

---

[2] See, e.g., *supra*, Chapter Three, notes 19, 21-22, 36-38.

[3] See *supra*, Chapter Four, notes 7-9.

of *the level of "genuine history"*? Our problem here is that differentiation of gospel traditions is a formidable task. Conceiving of separate levels is one matter; assigning individual traditions to a given level is another—for often no entirely objective and confident means are available for making such determinations. [4] Mark is not necessarily devoid of "solid historical fact," but the intermingling of layers of developing tradition and later redactional concerns makes it difficult to distinguish and disentangle the trustworthy from the questionable. Since, moreover, Mark did not share our modern concern with reliable historical reporting, to read Mark as historical testimony would be to misread him. Even accurate historical information he may have bequeathed to us was incidental to his theological interests and tailored to accommodate them.

Furthermore, even the three pre-Markan sources may reflect adaptation of traditions to the theological and socio-political needs of the early church. If so, our retreat to pre-redactional stages of the Gospel's composition will not necessarily bring into any clearer focus reliable historical traditions. For the sources we have proposed were primarily concerned with a presentation of Jesus, not a portrayal of the authority groups. The Jewish leaders functioned here merely as a foil for Jesus: conflict, or at least contrast, with Jesus was stressed; possible commonality—plausibly the case especially between Jesus and the scribes/Pharisees—was downplayed virtually altogether (except in 12:28-34a). For this reason, indeed, we find the whole controversy motif suspect to a degree. The controversy framework often served only a literary function. Teachings of Jesus not originally uttered within the context of a controversy may have been supplied with such a setting to render his words more vivid and to provide a model for conduct and response by later Christians in their encounters with the Pharisees of their day. Pre-Markan sources, accordingly, may convey more about the tensions of communities in which the collections were produced than about presumed historical confrontations involving Jesus himself. Moreover, just as Matthew and Luke introduced titles of Jewish leadership groups where Markan pericopae did not mention them, and just as Mark as well practiced interpolation (e.g., "scribes" in 1:22; 2:16; 3:22; 7:1, 5; "Pharisees" in 10:2), so even the compilers of the original collections may have introduced Jewish leadership groups into their still earlier traditions. [5]

---

[4] Cf. Achtemeier, *op. cit.*, 17ff.
[5] See, e.g., *supra*, Chapter Three, note 42; Chapter Four, notes 30, 51.

Factors such as these contribute to a skepticism. Jesus' alleged controversies with the Jewish leadership groups may not all originally have been controversies, and may not all originally have involved the Jewish leaders. We are not denying that Jesus engaged in controversies with Jewish authorities, but we are denying that Mark or his sources can be reliably used as a confirmation that such disputations occurred, or as a basis for reconstructing their substance or, even in some cases, as a means for identifying the disputants. The methodological difficulties we encounter in assessing all gospel traditions constitute the core of the particular problem of Jesus and the Jewish leaders in Mark. [6]

---

[6] Many scholars have expressed skepticism concerning the Markan controversy traditions. Some believe controversies actually occurred but feel that the descriptions of Jesus' opponents are distortions and that in reality Jesus shared much in common particularly with the scribes and Pharisees. See Moore, *op. cit.*, II, 193; Herford, *The Pharisees*, New York, 1924, 11-13; Marcus, *art. cit.*, 163; Lauterbach, 89. Jewish scholarship has tended to identify Pharisaism with Judaism and, accordingly, both to vindicate the scribes and Pharisees and to bring Jesus into proximity to them; see A. Geiger, *Das Judentum und seine Geschichte*, 2nd ed., Breslau, 1865, 117ff.; L. Stein, *Die Schrift des Lebens*, I, Strasbourg, 1872, 93ff.; H. Graetz, *History of the Jews*, II, Philadelphia, 1893, 148ff.; P. Goodman, *The Synagogue and the Church*, London, 1908, 238-241; K. Kohler, "The Pharisees," *JE*, IX, 661; G. Friedländer, *The Jewish Sources of the Sermon on the Mount*, repr., New York, 1969, 36, 94ff.; I. Abrahams, *Studies in Pharisaism and the Gospels*, Series 1-2, repr., New York, 1967; Klausner, *op. cit.*, 263-264, 288, 319, 365; A. Finkel, *op. cit.*, 130, 134, 172. Some scholars believe the controversy motifs are retrojections of tensions (especially over the Law) involving the later church rather than the historical Jesus; see Graetz, *Sinai et Golgotha, ou les origines du judaïsme et du christianisme...*, trans. M. Hess, Paris, 1867, 314-318, 392-407, 416-417; cf. *idem, History of the Jews*, II, 155f., 168-169; Riddle, *op. cit.*, 79, 106-109; A. Loisy, *The Origins of the New Testament*, trans. L. P. Jacks, London, 1950, 56-76, 80-81; L. E. Wright, *Alterations in the Words of Jesus...*, Cambridge, Mass., 1952; R. Graves and J. Podro, *The Nazarene Gospel Restored*, London, 1953, 3ff.; H. Mantel, *op. cit.*, 280-281; Sandmel, *Genius of Paul*, 38-39; and especially Winter, *op. cit.*, 113ff. Albertz himself admitted to many reservations: The order and interconnection of the controversies in Mark are not factual; the original core of a given disputation attracted later strata which the form critic must now peel away; the original oral stage of this material is beyond retrieval; the form of the controversies is basically unrealistic since streamlining of the episodes was needed so as to facilitate narration, inculcation and recall; and the sources underlying this material are so transparently sympathetic to Jesus' position that the disputes are highly artificial (*op. cit.*, 80-101). In spite of these concessions, however, Albertz persisted in accepting the controversy traditions (*Streitgespräche*) "als Niederschlag geschichtlicher Wirklichkeit" (*ibid.*, 64), a position generally upheld by Fascher, *op. cit.*, 149-150, 169; Easton, *Gospel before the Gospels*, 114-115; Grant, *Earliest Gospel*, 59-60; *idem, The Growth of the Gospels*, New York, 1933, Chapter V, esp. 105ff.; Taylor, *Formation*, 17, 37-38, 87; *idem, St. Mark*, 103; W. L. Knox, *op. cit.*, 14-16; see the survey of more recent similar views in D. Catchpole, *op. cit.*, 106ff. But the skeptics are the more convincing. See Bultmann's criticism of Albertz

The Distinctiveness of the Scribes and Pharisees in the Markan Treatment

Our analysis, therefore, makes no contribution on the level of the historical Jesus or his actual relations with the Jewish leaders. But is there something about the leadership groups themselves which we can learn from Mark? Of the five conspiratorial groups as presented by Mark, three do not merit serious attention by the historian. "Chief priests," "elders" and "Herodians" may be simply general constructs, not technical terms or precise descriptions of authority groups actually functioning in Jesus' day (or ever). Potentially, however, we might learn something significant from Mark about the scribes and Pharisees; for these two groups have surfaced at critical junctures in our study, leading us now to make the following observation: a series of passages peculiar to the Markan treatment distinguish the scribes and Pharisees from all the other Jewish authorities in such a way that these two groups alone have constituted both the core of the problems we have examined plus the nub of the solutions we have proposed. The distinctiveness of the scribes and Pharisees in Mark's overall presentation should thus arouse the historian's interest.

The scribes and Pharisees are first distinguished because Mark permits them the greatest degree of independence of all the conspiratorial groups. We have already indicated [7] that neither Herodians nor elders ever appear by themselves and that, for all intents and purposes, the same is true of the chief priests. Only the scribes and the Pharisees can appear without their respective allies. This freedom of movement and of appearance allows scribes and Pharisees to become the sole exceptions to Mark's otherwise rigidly compartmentalized scheme of two separate camps of conspirators.

Secondly, scribes and Pharisees are distinctive in that they are the only groups to trouble Jesus in a variety of ways. The harassment of Jesus by Jewish leaders expresses itself in different forms in Mark: conspiracy to have Jesus killed, and confrontation with Jesus, questioning him especially either about his denigration of the Law of Moses or about the adequacy of his messianic credentials. Three of the groups are active almost exclusively in the first respect: chief priests, elders,

---

(op. cit., 40 n. 1) and also the detailed analysis of many of the controversy pericopae (40-54, 67). Also J. Neusner, From Politics to Piety: the Emergence of Pharisaic Judaism, Englewood Cliffs, N.J., 1973, 67ff.

[7] See supra, Chapter Three, notes 10-12.

and Herodians. [8] But the Pharisees are active in *two* respects, the conspiracy and the matter of legalism, [9] and the scribes in all *three*. [10] A puzzle emerges as well: Whenever the terms "scribes" and "Pharisees" appear together, [11] both authority groups are in disputation with Jesus over the matter of the Law; whenever engaged in plotting Jesus' destruction, [12] however, the scribes and the Pharisees never conspire together but are always conjoined instead with their respective allies —the chief priests + elders, on the one hand, and the Herodians, on the other. And whenever Jesus' messianic credentials are under discussion, [13] the Pharisees are absent. Why do the scribes and Pharisees readily join forces on the issue of the Law but never on either of the other matters?

Furthermore, some Jewish conspiratorial groups in Mark are rooted in specific geographic environs. Jesus encounters the chief priests and elders only in Jerusalem itself. [14] The Herodians, meanwhile, must be associated with Galilee only, if our view of 12:13ff. is correct. [15]

---

[8] This is essentially the case with the chief priests and the elders in all their appearances (but cf. *infra*, note 24). As for the Herodians, they plot Jesus' destruction in 3:6. While, in 12:13ff., the Herodians are indeed involved in *legal* dispute with Jesus, the legal point at issue is not related to the Law of Moses but rather Caesar's right to tribute. Moreover, since 12:13 must be read in conjunction with 3:6, as we have already shown, Mark intends the reader to know that, whatever the issue at stake in 12:13ff., the Herodians are bent on destroying Jesus. Nor should the Herodians in 3:6 be regarded as involved in legal disputation. They are absent from the controversy in 3:1-5: those disputing Jesus here are solely the Pharisees who subsequently go out to hold "counsel with the Herodians against him, how to destroy him." Moreover, as we have indicated, 3:6 may originally have completed 12:13-17, 34b rather than 3:1-5.

[9] The Pharisees plot his destruction in 3:6 (cf. 12:13ff.), and confront him over the Law in, e.g., 2:18ff.; 2:23ff.; 3:1-5 (that Jesus' opponents here are Pharisees is inferred from the juxtaposition of 3:1-5 with 2:23-28); 7:1ff.; etc.

[10] The scribes are involved in legal confrontation with Jesus in 2:16ff. and 7:1ff. They plot his destruction in 14:1 and subsequent passages of the Passion narrative; cf. 8:31; 10:33; 11:18, 27. They question his credentials especially in 9:11ff. and 12:35ff.

[11] Mk. 2:16; 7:1, 5.

[12] See *supra*, notes 9-10.

[13] See *supra*, note 10.

[14] He alludes to chief priests and elders in 8:31, and to chief priests again in 10:33, but does not encounter them until his entry to Jerusalem in Chapter 11, verses 18, 27.

[15] It is natural to infer that "Herodians" were associated by Mark with Herod Antipas of Galilee; also, quite naturally, "Herodians" became a variant reading for "Herod" in Mk. 8:15, especially under the influence of the text in 3:6 and 12:13. The Pharisees with whom the Herodians conspire must also have been considered by Mark Galilean since he makes scribes come down from Jerusalem to meet them; in this respect also, therefore, Herodians, their allies, seem Galilean. In our view, the appearance of Herodians in Jerusalem in Mk. 12:13ff. is misleading: 12:13-17,

But the scribes and Pharisees are again distinguished—Mark shows them appearing, both individually and jointly, in both Galilee and also Judaea. [16]

The Interest of Historians in the Scribes and Pharisees

These several perplexities, therefore, explain why the scribes and Pharisees are to *us* the most interesting Jewish leadership groups in the Markan treatment. Scribes and Pharisees have also been the most engrossing to other scholars, though for different reasons altogether. Today, for example, it is commonly understood how important Pharisaism initially was in the evolution of ongoing Judaism, and this alone has occasioned many studies of its origins and development. Of course, Pharisaism was not the only mode of Palestinian Judaism in the time of Jesus, but it was the only mode to survive in a meaningful way the destruction of the Temple in the year 70 C.E. It was, therefore, a force to be reckoned with during the period when the Evangelists themselves were completing their gospels—not to mention in earlier decades when Mark's sources on the Jewish leaders must have come into being.

Some scholars believe, moreover, that we can best compare Christianity and Judaism by juxtaposing the gospels with the earliest teachings imbedded in rabbinic literature: in so far as is possible, Jesus' sayings should be evaluated in the light of the teachings of his Pharisaic contemporaries. And since Mark (and therefore the later Synoptists as well) depicts the Pharisees in such close association with the scribes, without drawing any meaningful distinction between the two groups, those scholars already interested in the Pharisees naturally gravitate toward the scribes as well.

Two problems in particular have stimulated scholarly interest: How should we use our sources in defining the scribes and Pharisees of

---

34b was originally juxtaposed to what is now 3:1-5, in a Galilean setting. Luke also presumed Herodians were Galilean. Mark's statement in 12:13 that Herodians were present in Jerusalem occasioned Luke's portrayal of Herod Antipas' arrival in Jerusalem from Galilee (Lk. 23:6ff.). Cf. also *supra*, Chapter Two, note 17; Chapter Three, note 33.

[16] Scribes appear outside Judaea (in, e.g., 2:6, 16; 3:22; 7:1, 5; 9:14); they appear as well in Jerusalem (11:18, 27; 12:28, 32; 14:1, 43, 53; 15:1, 31) from which they are twice said to come into Galilee (3:22; 7:1). Pharisees appear in Galilee in, e.g., 2:18, 24; 3:6; 7:1, 5; they also meet Jesus as soon as he crosses into Judaea (10:2), and appear in Jerusalem once later (12:13). Actually, as we have explained, these impressions are only superficial; the Pharisees' presence in Judaea is editorial just as is the scribes' presence in Galilee.

Jesus' day? How should we use our sources in defining Jesus' relations with the scribes and Pharisees? The inability of scholars to reach a consensus on these two issues has had the effect of stimulating ever new analyses and hypotheses. As we have detailed elsewhere, [17] our difficulties here issue mainly from the nature of our sources—sources which are susceptible of varying interpretations which, in turn, yield varying reconstructions.

On the matter of defining the Pharisees, each of our three sources—rabbinic literature, Josephus and the New Testament—manifests a general bias: either supportive of them or antithetical towards them. These biases impede our attempts at objective definition; it becomes a complicated task determining how best to balance the generally positive orientation toward Pharisees in Josephus and rabbinic literature with the predominantly negative disposition toward them manifested by the Synoptists. At the same time, each of our sources is to a degree internally inconsistent in defining the Pharisees. [18] Rabbinic literature and Josephus, moreover, date from after 70 C.E., as do the four gospels and Acts, with the result that it is unclear whether the descriptions of the Pharisees therein contained reflect the pre-70 period—as is often commonly presumed—or instead represent retrojections of the more mature image of the Pharisees/rabbis from the Jamnia period or later. Pauline testimony on Pharisaism, meanwhile, while definitely pre-70, is minimal, and Luke's description of Paul's Pharisaism is problematic. [19]

Consequently, scholars defining the Pharisees are divided on even the most fundamental of issues: First, did the Pharisees wish to extend the ritual restrictions of the sacrificial cult to the populace at large, and thereby to transform all society into "a kingdom of priests"? Or did they instead intend to saddle the priesthood only with such burdens,

---

[17] See our forthcoming study, "Jesus and the Pharisees: the Problem as It Stands Today," *JES* 15 (Summer 1978; tentative).

[18] Thus, while Josephus is usually favorably disposed toward the Pharisees (espec. *Antiq.* XVIII.i.3 [xviii.12-17]; *Life* 2 [12]), occasionally he is less adulatory or even critical of them (e.g., *Antiq.* XIII.xv.5 [xiii.408-410]; *War* I.v.2 [i.110-114]). While the gospels are usually condemnatory of the Pharisees, occasionally Luke in particular shows them in a more positive light (e.g., Lk. 13:31; Acts 5:34f.). Rabbinic literature, meanwhile, though virtually always favorable toward the Pharisees, may be understood as occasionally censuring them; see, e.g., Moore, "Christian Writers on Judaism," *HTR* 14 (1921), 238; H. Loewe, "Pharisaism," *Judaism and Christianity*, I, 186 n. 1; and especially Rivkin, *art. cit.*

[19] See *supra*, Chapter One, note 21, and especially Sandmel, *Genius of Paul*, 13ff., 44ff.

freeing the common people from an inflexible Sadducean interpretation of the Law? [20] Secondly, are we to presume that the Pharisees,
arising from the lower classes, involved in secular trades, active in the
synagogue, were therefore beloved of the masses? Or would their
popularity inevitably have been compromised given their preoccupation
with ritual and tithing and their consequent resentment of the many
who ignored the laws of Levitical purity? How we resolve this second
matter may hinge upon how we respond to the first. Thirdly, were
the Pharisees themselves all learned in the Law or, instead, only the
relatively unlearned lay adherents of the scribes, their learned elite?
(And were the scribes the learned elite of the Pharisees?) Fourthly,
were the Pharisees in Jesus' time mostly concerned with ritual piety
and table fellowship, and hence withdrawn from political activism,
or were their interests instead considerably broader and their activity
more political in orientation? [21] Even the finest studies on the Pharisees
offer noticeable contrasts on these most fundamental matters of definition. [22] Accordingly, with no consensus on defining the Pharisees there
can be no consensus on defining the Pharisees' relations with Jesus.
And what is true with the Markan Pharisees is true with the Markan
scribes as well; even though the scholarship here is less voluminous,
there has yet persisted considerable variety of opinion. [23]

Scribes and Pharisees in Mark: The Significance of Our Proposals

What does our study contribute toward the redirection of the
scholarship on the scribes and Pharisees?

1. *Accounting for the distinctiveness of scribes and Pharisees in
Mark.* We have called attention to a number of perplexities in Mark's
treatment of the scribes and Pharisees. We now explain them as follows:

---

[20] For especially characteristic statements of the first position, see Jeremias, *op. cit.*,
247ff.; Branscomb, *op. cit.*, 50ff. A forerunner of the second position was A. Geiger,
Urschrift und Übersetzungen der Bibel, Frankfurt a.M., 1928, 101-158; see also
J. Z. Lauterbach, *Rabbinic Essays*, 95-96; Marcus, *art. cit.*, 158; S. Zeitlin, *The Rise
and Fall of the Judaean State*, I, Philadelphia, 1964, 179ff. Scholars who have combined elements of both approaches include Herford, *The Pharisees*; Finkelstein,
op. cit.; G. Allon, *Meḥqarim be-Toledot Yisrael*, Tel Aviv, 1957, I, 176.
[21] Important discussions on this problem are those by J. Neusner, *The Rabbinic
Traditions about the Pharisees before 70*, 3 vols., Leiden, 1971 (hence the title of his
abridged popularization: *From Politics to Piety: the Emergence of Pharisaic Judaism*),
and Allon, *op. cit.*, I, 26-47. See further discussion, *infra.*
[22] Compare the positions of Neusner, *Rabbinic Traditions*, and Rivkin, *art. cit.*
See our comments on these approaches in "Jesus and the Pharisees...," note 38.
[23] See *supra*, Chapter Four, notes 39-43.

Scribes and Pharisees emerge as the most independent of the leadership groups in Mark for several reasons. First, one of Mark's three sources on the Jewish authorities focused on the scribes; accordingly, in pericopae in Mark derived from this source (12:18-34a; 9:11-12a, 13ab; 12:35-40), we often find the scribes appearing independently. Secondly, scribes were the one group from the Jerusalem triad whom Mark comfortably could retroject into Galilee, and his practice of interpolating scribes into pericopae in Chapters 1-9 (e.g., 1:22; 2:6; 3:22; 9:14) explains why scribes in these instances now appear independently. Thirdly, in some pericopae in the pre-Markan Pharisee/Herodian collection, Pharisees appeared alone, and pericopae in the canonical Mark derived from this source now preserve the impression of their independence. Thus, for example, Pharisees now appear independently in 2:23ff. and, implicitly, in 3:1-5; and originally the same was true in 2:15ff. and 7:1ff. (before Mark himself interpolated "scribes" into these texts in 2:16 and 7:1, 5). Fourthly, Pharisees were also available, as an independent group, for ready interpolation elsewhere, especially as in 10:2 (where an aspect of the Law was under dispute).

The reason why scribes and Pharisees are the only exceptions to the otherwise rigid compartmentalization of the leadership groups has already been detailed in Chapter Four: Mark interpolated scribes into many pericopae in Chapters 1-9, and two such pericopae (2:15ff.; 7:1ff.) were derived from the pre-Markan Pharisee/Herodian collection; hence "Pharisees" were *already* present in them. "Scribes" were in this fashion brought into contact with "Pharisees," these the sole instances wherein the boundary line between the two camps of conspirators was crossed by a leadership group.

Mark's dependence on three sources also accounts for the different patterns of harassment to which Jesus seems subject in Mark. In the early Passion tradition, chief priests + scribes + elders are cast in a distinctly political role; they do not dispute with Jesus over his views on the Law of Moses or over doctrinal matters. [24] Elsewhere in Mark, however, we do find *scribes* (appearing alone) voicing doctrinal concerns to which Jesus makes response; this circumstance arises from

---

[24] The dispute between Jesus and the high priest in the Sanhedrin is not part of the early Passion tradition (see *supra*, Chapter Three, note 12, Chapter Four, notes 8-9, and *infra*, note 38). The presence of chief priests during the Question on Authority is editorial; in this respect, 11:27 is like 8:31; 10:33-34; 11:18, as we have indicated in Chapter Four.

Mark's dependence on his scribe collection (12:18-34a; 9:11-12a, 13ab; 12:35-40)—dealing with matters of resurrection, the greatest teachings, the anticipation of Elijah's advance coming, the question of the Messiah's Davidic ancestry (with an addendum: the behavior inappropriate to those holding the office of scribe). The reason that scribes harass Jesus in still a third respect—on the issue of the Law—is *solely* that Mark has interpolated scribes into two Pharisee pericopae (2:15ff.; 7:1ff.); indeed, the Pharisee/Herodian collection dealt *mainly* with the issue of the Law, reflecting the type of opposition which the Pharisees (and later the rabbis) brought to bear against Christian missionaries. In the original traditions of dialogue between Jesus and scribes, however, Jesus voiced no denigration of the Law—perhaps because the issue of the Law had yet to be raised in the church. We see Jesus' negative statements on the Law as late attributions, postdating both him and the special scribe collection as well, but included in the later Pharisee/Herodian source. [25]

Finally, Mark's dependence on three sources also explains why most of the leadership groups are rooted, respectively, in only one geographical region. The early Passion tradition placed chief priests + scribes + elders in Judaea (specifically Jerusalem). Mark's special source on the scribes either was already set in Jerusalem or Mark, identifying *these* scribes with those from the Jerusalem triad, naturally presumed that the special scribe traditions should likewise be set in Jerusalem. Herodians, meanwhile, were associated by Mark with Herod Antipas, and so understood as Galilean-based; naturally, therefore, he construed their Pharisaic allies as likewise Galilean. [26] Since, however, in accommodating his sources to one another, Mark retrojected the Jerusalem scribes into Galilee, scribes came to be a group making appearances in *both* regions, Galilee as well as Judaea. Similarly, Pharisees came to appear in both regions: on one occasion, Mark shifted Pharisees from Galilee into Jerusalem (by detaching and transferring what is now 12:13-17, 34b from its original juxtaposition to 3:1-5) and, in a preparatory instance (10:2), he interpolated Pharisees into Judaea so that Jesus could encounter them immediately upon his entry into that region.

So much then for the perplexities we have noted and the solutions we have proposed. Let us turn now to other matters of concern to the historian.

---

[25] Consult listings, *supra*, note 6.
[26] See also, *supra*, note 15.

2. *Defining the scribes and Pharisees and their relation to one another.* Our analysis stimulates the following thought: While we cannot demonstrate that "scribes" and "Pharisees" are absolutely synonymous terms, it is significant that the need to distinguish between the two no longer seems so compelling.

Two popular notions—a) that the scribes in the time of Jesus were a subgroup of the Pharisees (perhaps their intellectual elite) and 2) that the Sadducees also had their own scribes—both take their cue from Acts 23:9 in conjunction with three verses from Mark (primarily 2:16 ["the scribes of the Pharisees"]; also 7:1, 5). But Acts 23:9 ("then a great clamor arose; and some of the scribes of the Pharisees' party stood up and contended, 'We find nothing wrong in this man...' ") is hardly historically reliable. As we have indicated in Chapter Two, we feel Luke was unsure who scribes were; for his comprehension of them, he relied heavily on Mark (and possibly on Matthew as well). Did he have any other source on "scribes" which could have supplied him with the notion that scribes were a subdivision of Pharisees? Scholars know of no other such source. We feel it is possible that 23:9 was Luke's own construction based on what he inferred from Mark. [27]

We conjecture that Acts 23:9 evolved in the following fashion: Luke often paralleled episodes in the life of Paul with those from the life of Jesus; [28] in their respective trials in particular, each defendant is unjustly charged by Jewish accusers but later is adjudged innocent by the Roman magistrate. But the account of Paul's trial incorporates a second Markan motif as well: a dispute with the Sadducees over the doctrine of resurrection (Mk. 12:18-28). Resurrection was a key issue of contention between Sadducees and *Pharisees*; the Markan controversy between Jesus and the Sadducees could well be an adaptation of a Sadducee-Pharisee encounter, with Jesus introduced as espousing the

---

[27] The usual meaning of *grammateus* in Classical Greek is "a secretary" or "registrar"; in the LXX a kind of public officer or "clerk of works" (Exod. 5:6) or a low-ranking military officer who was a keeper of records (Deut. 20:5). "Scribes" in Markan usage do not seem reminiscent of this usual understanding of the term. Nor does the word *grammateus* or *grammateis* in Josephan usage seem analogous to "scribes" mentioned so frequently in Mark. The term usually appears in the singular, apparently in the sense of a secretary or clerk or assistant to a superior (cf. *Antiq.* XI.vi.10 [xi.248]; X.iv.1 [x.55]). See also *infra*, note 41. Since Luke's description of scribes bears resemblance to that in Mark but not to that of other sources, we suspect Mark was his fundamental source here.

[28] See A. J. Mattill, Jr., "The Jesus-Paul Parallels and the Purpose of Luke-Acts: H. H. Evans Reconsidered," *NovT* 17 (1975), 15-46.

Pharisaic position. But Mark counters the Sadducees with Jesus *and* a *scribe* (12:28) and does not mention *Pharisees* at all.

Now ordinarily, in presenting Paul's trial, Luke could have used "Pharisees" alone to oppose Sadducees, as he seems intent on doing in 23:7-8. In Luke's own day, it must have been common knowledge that Pharisees espoused a doctrine of resurrection; and, if Luke utilized Josephus, his awareness of this would have been all the more secure. In any event, Luke would have had at least three options in describing the dispute over resurrection during Paul's trial: a) he could have identified the disputants as Sadducees and *Pharisees* (relying on common knowledge and possibly Josephus as well; see 23:7-8); b) he could have identified the disputants as Sadducees and *scribes* (relying on Mk. 12:28, which presented the position of the scribe[s] on this particular issue, and also on 14:53, which established the membership of the scribes in the Sanhedrin); or c) in some fashion or another, he could have identified the opponents of the Sadducees as *both Pharisees and scribes* (the option he preferred in 23:9).

But having chosen the last option in 23:9, why did he prefer the particular formulation "scribes of the Pharisees' party"? We propose that, in Luke's edition of Mark, the reading of 2:16 was "scribes of the Pharisees," the *lectio difficilior* (which some other manuscripts corrected to "scribes and Pharisees"). Whether this was the original reading in Mark we cannot determine: 7:1, 5 seems to represent Mark's basic understanding; "scribes of the Pharisees" may be an error even though present in Luke's early copy of Mark. This passage induced Luke to use, in Acts 23:9, the peculiar phrase "scribes of the Pharisees' party." In this fashion, Luke could oppose the Sadducees with the Pharisees (as would ordinarily have been expected) and also with scribes (as per Mk. 12:28), and yet have the Sadducees opposed by one group ("scribes of the Pharisees' party") rather than a more unwieldy two ("scribes *and* Pharisees").

Many modern scholars, however, not here suspecting Luke's possible dependence on Mk. 2:16, have construed Acts 23:9 as corroborating the relation of scribes to Pharisees specified in that Markan verse. Both expressions—"scribes of the Pharisees" and "scribes of the Pharisees' party"—are thereupon commonly cited to "prove" that *Sadducees* also must have had *their* scribes: Otherwise, it is reasoned, if *all* scribes were Pharisaic, then Mark (in 2:16) and Luke (in Acts 23:9) could have used "scribes" alone; allegedly, the additional phrase, *of the Pharisees(' party)*, was intended to distinguish *these* scribes from scribes presumably *of the Sadducees or of the Sadducees' party.*

If our overall analysis is correct, however, then of course this last bit of reasoning is fallacious. Should Luke here be dependent on Mark, then Acts 23:9 furnishes no corroboration of the relation of scribes to Pharisees as specified in those manuscripts of Mark 2:16 reading "scribes of the Pharisees." And Mk. 2:16 would itself be misleading —for, in our view, all three verses in Mark linking scribes to Pharisees (2:16; 7:1, 5) do not depict any genuinely historical relation between these two groups; in each case, the juxtaposition issues from Mark's interpolation of scribes into pericopae where they were not initially present! In our judgment, therefore, the Synoptists provide no information whatsoever either that scribes were a subdivision of Pharisees or that the Sadducees as well as Pharisees had scribes.

One might infer, therefore, that we should now dissociate scribes from Pharisees altogether since it is Mark alone who has brought them together. But, ironically, this very circumstance enhances the possibility that "scribes" and "Pharisees" were synonymous. Two considerations are instructive here: First, scholars dismissing the possibility that "scribes" and "Pharisees" were synonymous take their cue from Mk. 7:1, 5 (verses which present them as if they were distinct from one another) and Mk. 2:16 plus Acts 23:9 (verses which depict scribes as a subdivision of Pharisees). But we have argued that these verses are useless to the historian; the distinctions they propose between scribes and Pharisees surface only on the level of redaction; they do not reside on the early (and possibly hypothetical) level of "solid historical fact." Secondly, we believe Mark would have presented scribes and Pharisees as distinct groups even if they were in reality identical! For Mark's two sources which mentioned "scribes" never once mentioned "Pharisees," and his one source which mentioned "Pharisees" never once mentioned "scribes"; since "scribes" and "Pharisees" never appeared *together* in any of his three sources on the Jewish leaders, the *possibility* of their synonymity may not have occurred to Mark. Accordingly, even while he was unable to discern any substantive difference between "scribes" and "Pharisees," he naturally would have presumed that persons referred to by two different titles must have been two distinct groups, and he would have presented them accordingly. This means, therefore, that Mark's presentation of scribes and Pharisees as distinct groups in no way reduces the *possibility* of their actual synonymity. This is the ambiguity which seems to leave Matthew so perplexed with Mark, such that seven times in Chapter 23 he considers scribes and Pharisees to be distinct groups even though the offenses he attributes to the one group are precisely those he blames on the other. Nor is it surprising that Luke, having no clue as to how to distinguish scribes from Pharisees, defines them in terms of what they have in common. And of course it is hardly unexpected that many modern scholars rely on the same four verses (Mk. 2:16; 7:1, 5; Acts 23:9) when they define the relation of scribes to Pharisees.

Neither of the popular notions we have cited, therefore, is convincingly founded: There really is no evidence that scribes mentioned in the gospels were a subdivision of the Pharisees. And the Synoptists furnish no reliable indication that the Sadducees had scribes; this notion is merely an inference based on Mk. 2:16 and Acts 23:9, [29] the latter verse dependent on the former, and the former itself artificial in construction. But more remains to be said on the matter of Sadducean scribes.

3. *The two images of scribes in Mark.* Two types of scribes appear in Mark, and they contrast strongly with one another: we find some scribes who seem specifically Pharisaic in their orientation (especially in 1:22; 2:6, 16; 3:22; 7:1, 5; 9:11, 14; 12:28, 32, 35, 38), and also other scribes who, because they are allied with the chief priests, could be construed as Sadducean (in 8:31; 10:33; 11:18, 27; 14:1, 43, 53; 15:1, 31). [30] On this basis, whenever scribes are involved in disputation with Jesus over the Law or the validity of his credentials, we should presume them to be Pharisaic; and whenever they are active in political conspiracy to have Jesus arrested or executed, we could consider them Sadducean.

But we need not have recourse to "Sadducean scribes" in order to explain the two contrasting images of scribes in Mark. "Scribes" appeared in two of Mark's three sources on the Jewish leadership groups: In the special scribe collection (underlying 12:18-34a; 9:11-12a, 13ab; 12:35-40), the image of scribes is definitely Pharisaic; in the pre-Markan Passion tradition, the image of scribes is not Sadducean but rather *indistinct* altogether. Hence arose the two contrasting images of scribes in Mark.

Finding "scribes" mentioned in two of his sources, naturally Mark

---

[29] Cf. *infra*, note 41.

[30] See Klausner, *op. cit.*, especially 317ff., 334-335. Since he cannot explain why scribes in 11:18, 27 and Chapters 14-15 seem so different from those in Chapters 1-3, 7, 9, and 12, he abruptly introduces Sadducean scribes when Jesus reaches Jerusalem.

identified the scribes from the one source with the scribes from the other. Thus it is that, when Mark realized that the scribes were the only Jerusalem-based group he could retroject from Judaea into Galilee, he used the information about the scribes from his special scribe collection to assist him in retrojecting the scribes from the Passion tradition's triad. Perhaps Mark was correct here: even though the images of "scribes" in these two sources seem so different from one another, there is no actual basis for dissociating the scribes in the one source from the scribes in the other. Possibly, the differences in the two descriptions of the scribes arise from the difference in subjects treated in the two sources or the difference in the concerns of the compilers. The scribes mentioned in the Passion source could have been Pharisees even though their image there is so ill-defined, and even though the term "Pharisees" is never mentioned there.

4. *The absence of the Pharisees from the Passion narrative.* Are Pharisees absent from the Passion narrative because they played no role in Jesus' arrest or trial? Some historians do indeed presume that Pharisees (and hence Pharisaic scribes) of Jesus' day were withdrawn from politics. [31] Accordingly, Pharisees could have readily badgered Jesus over religious—i.e., legal or doctrinal—issues, but quite possibly they took no part in the political conspiracy hatched by the Jerusalem triad: chief priests + scribes + elders. On the assumption that the Pharisees were withdrawn from the political sphere of that time, some scholars may feel constrained to define the scribes in the Jerusalem triad as something other than Pharisaic (e.g., "Sadducean scribes" or simply "civil servants"). While later Evangelists did indeed introduce Pharisees into their Passion narratives, we can discount these additions as a reflection of their later context. In their day, not only was Pharisaism perceived as a major Jewish force opposing the church, but the Sadducees and the priesthood had faded considerably from the popular memory; these factors encouraged the introduction of "Pharisees" into sections of the gospel from which they had been absent in Mark. [32]

---

[31] E.g., Morton Smith, "Palestinian Judaism in the First Century," in *Israel: Its Role in Civilization*, ed. Moshe Davis, New York, 1956, 75-77, followed by Neusner, *From Politics to Piety*, 64ff.

[32] E.g., Mt. 27:62; see also Chwolson, *op. cit.*, 113, on Mt. 27:41; cf. Jn. 11:47, 57; 18:3. Some scholars have argued that many gospel traditions originally dealt with "Sadducees" and "[Sadducean] scribes" and that "Pharisees" and "[Pharisaic] scribes" were, respectively, substituted for them by later copyists or by the Evangelists themselves. See Chwolson, 112ff.; Büchler, *op. cit.*, 80-87; cf. also Olmstead, *op. cit.*, 178ff.

Can we really be certain, however, that the Pharisees before 70 were so entirely withdrawn from the political arena and that this explains their absence from the Passion narrative? As we have proposed, much of the Pharisee material in Mark comes from a pre-70 source underlying 7:1ff.; 2:15-3:5; 12:13-17, 34b; 3:6. And most of the concerns of the Pharisees in these passages do indeed relate to what can be termed table-fellowship and the laws of ritual purity and piety. But the distinction between authority in religious matters and at least influence in politics is a fine one. Are we seriously to believe that a group eschewing politics before 70 underwent so profound a meta-morphosis that after 70 it was suddenly deemed by Rome equipped to assume the reins of political leadership? [33] What induced Rome to elevate the Pharisees to power if they were a group having demon-strated no political ambition, influence or aptitude before 70? Some have suggested Josephus was instrumental in their being boosted to power; more likely, however, his Pharisaic partisanship reflects his desire to be associated with this newly empowered group, not his attempt *ab initio* to persuade Rome of their importance. [34]

In our own analysis, we have noted that at least twice in the pre-Markan Pharisee/Herodian collection Pharisees are considered allies of the Herodians, [35] the latter clearly to be conceived of as a political rather than a religious force; [36] quite possibly the term is to be under-stood in conjunction with Herod Antipas. "Herodians" were integral to this source; they were not introduced by Mark. It is true that, elsewhere, Mark did interpolate titles of the Jewish conspiratorial groups, especially "scribes" and "Pharisees." But "Herodians" was a title problematic to Mark and the later Synoptists as well. As we have shown in Chapter Two, no Evangelist seemed to know who "Herod-ians" were; the tendency of each was, clearly, to drop the title, not to interpolate it. Accordingly, the notion in 3:6 and 12:13 (cf. 8:15) that Pharisees were naturally allied with or could reasonably be juxta-posed to Herodians must reflect a pre-70 perspective; at that time, in other words, there seemed nothing anomalous about portraying the

[33] Cf., e.g., R. Scroggs, "The Earliest Christian Communities as Sectarian Move-ment," *Christianity, Judaism and Other Greco-Roman Cults: Studies for Morton Smith at Sixty*, ed. J. Neusner, Part Two, Leiden, 1975, 11 n. 39.
[34] Cf. Smith, *op. cit.*, 75-76.
[35] Mk. 3:6; 12:13; cf. 8:15.
[36] Almost all attempts to define the "Herodians" view them in political terms; see the listings, *supra*, Chapter Two, notes 6-7.

Pharisees as politically active and influential (regardless of what their prime interests genuinely happened to be).

We therefore believe the "Pharisees" are absent from the Passion narrative not because they were withdrawn from the political sphere in the early first century, but only because the early Passion traditions received by Mark never mentioned Pharisees *under that title*. But this source did mention "scribes" in addition to "chief priests" + "elders." Were these scribes Pharisees? Scribes in 12:18-34a; 9:11-12a, 13ab; 12:35-40 were indubitably Pharisaic; if the Pharisees were not totally withdrawn from the political arena, could their presence not be implicit in the Passion narrative under the rubric "scribes"?

Of course, since the scribes here seem such ready allies of the chief priests, the comfortable assumption is that they were Sadducean. But we have argued that there is no evidence supporting the convenient notion that the term "scribes" here or anywhere in the Synoptists means "Sadducean scribes." Moreover, must we dismiss the idea that "Pharisees" and "chief priests" could function in partnership? Groups divided on ideological grounds can unite on less controversial matters: on doctrinal issues, scribes (= Pharisees) might have shared little with "chief priests"; but on the matter of arresting a possible subversive against Rome, cooperation might have been readily forthcoming.

Another alternative presents itself: that the term "scribes" *in the Passion narrative* is only a literary device. Of the three groups in the Jerusalem triad, the chief priests (i.e., priestly elements) are the most credible as agents of Jesus' arrest. [37] The mentions of "scribes" and "elders," however, actually inspire only little confidence. We believe these two groups were present in the pre-Markan Passion tradition, but even there they served an apologetic function: to flesh out a fuller and hence more impressive enemy contingent so as, thereby, to aggrandize the image of Jesus himself, their target. For indeed this is all the scribes and elders seem to do—they are merely tagalongs of the chief priests, having no independence and performing no distinctive mission of their own. Since the term "scribes" as *here* used is so amorphous, it is conceivably the same kind of general construct as "chief priests," "elders," and "Herodians." If this is the case, then any attempt to define "scribes" in the Passion narrative would be misdirected.

It would also be ill-advised to inquire concerning the nature of the Sanhedrin interrogating Jesus, with the aim of inferring therefrom the

---

[37] See, e.g., Sloyan, *op. cit.*, 128.

type of scribe likely to have been a member. We are so unclear concerning the nature of this institution in the time of Jesus; accordingly, even if scribes did belong to this body—and of this we have no assurance—we would have no way of determining who they were. Moreover, the Sanhedrin episode in Mark inspires no confidence: it does not belong to the early Passion tradition, and indeed there is no assurance that Jesus ever appeared before any such body. [38]

Are other sources of help? What "scribe" means in Ezra [39] or Ben Sira [40] is not necessarily useful since both writings are pre-Pharisaic and, in any event, deal with a context centuries earlier than Mark. Josephus, meanwhile, does not speak of "scribes" with any frequency or present them as a leadership group. [41] But the term does appear in rabbinic sources (sopherim), at times even used interchangeably with "Pharisees" (perushim [42]) and rabbinic "sages" (hakhamim). [43] Con-

---

[38] Many studies of the Sanhedrin (or Sanhedrins) in Jesus' day attempt to reconcile the apparent discrepancies between the portrait of the Sanhedrin offered by Josephus and the gospels, on the one hand, and the court described in detail in rabbinic literature, on the other. Major options include the following: a) The Greek sources describe the Sanhedrin in an earlier period, during the time of Jesus, while the Hebrew/Aramaic sources reflect the Sanhedrin during a later period. b) There were essentially two types of Sanhedrin operative simultaneously in Jesus' day, the Greek sources describing a political court, the Hebrew/Aramaic sources presenting a religious court. c) The testimony of both the gospels and rabbinic literature is suspect, and hence the problem posed by the discrepancies ceases to be significant: the Sanhedrin's procedures as described in rabbinic literature emerge as something of an idealization and hence there is doubt as to whether they were ever even operative; and, for that matter, questions exist as to whether Jesus himself was ever really tried before a Jewish Sanhedrin. Helpful presentations of these positions include: Burkill, "Sanhedrin," *IDB*, IV; Mantel, *op. cit.*, and "Sanhedrin," *IDB* Suppl. Vol.; Zeitlin, *op. cit.*, I, 202-212; Rivkin, "Beth Din, Boulé, Sanhedrin: A Tragedy of Errors," *HUCA* 46 (1975), 181-199; H. Danby, "The Bearing of the Rabbinical Criminal Code on the Jewish Trial Narratives in the Gospels," *JTS* 21 (1919), 51-76; Achtemeier, *op. cit.*, 88ff.; Donahue, *Are You the Christ?*
[39] Ezra 7:6, 11, 12; cf. Neh. 8:4, 9, 13; 12:26, 36.
[40] Ecclesiasticus 38:24-39:15.
[41] See *supra*, n. 27. M. Black calls attention to "one inconclusive reference in Josephus (War VI.v.3) to *hierogrammateis*, where the context appears to favor 'priestly scribes.' But it is also possible to explain Josephus' term as a general description of Jewish scribes, intended for Greek readers, without any particular reference to priestly or Sadducean scribes. The Sanhedrin scribes may have been entirely Pharisees..." (*IDB*, IV, s.v. "Scribe," 247).
[42] I.e., where the term *perushim* refers to the class of teachers knowledgable in the two-fold Law of Moses, not where *perushim* refers to "separatists," "ascetics," "fanatics," etc. The clearest study of these passages is by Rivkin, "Defining the Pharisees...."
[43] For an example of such interchangeable usage, see Rivkin's analysis of *Yadayim* 3:5 (an anonymous teaching), *Yadayim* 4:6 (where the same teaching is attributed

ceivably, *sopherim* was a term used by the *ḥakhamim* to refer to their forerunners. [44] Possibly in the Gospel's Passion traditions, and quite probably in the special scribe collection, "scribes" represents an early term of reference to Pharisees; "Pharisees" is a common term in the time when, and the place where, the later material, Stratum III, was formulated; this body of traditions dealt almost entirely with the issue of the validity of the Written and Oral Law, a problem occasioned by the influence of Pauline teachings. [45]

To end, however, on a note with which we began: our primary concern should be not with our own understanding of who the leadership groups were but with the Evangelists' understanding about these groups and with the understanding of those compiling the sources they used. So even if the "scribes" in the Passion narrative were only a construct, or civil servants, or Sadducees, we nevertheless believe that *Mark* viewed them as identical with the "scribes" in the pre-Markan scribe collection. Had he realized that "scribes" in this latter collection were synonymous with "Pharisees," he very likely would have perceived the "scribes" in the Passion tradition also as Pharisaic; and he may then even have felt disposed to introduce the term "Pharisees" into

---

to the *perushim*), and *Yadayim* 3:2 (where the same dictum turns out to have been sponsored by the *sopherim*). Accordingly, *perushim* and *sopherim* appear synonymous, and, since anonymous teachings often represent the viewpoint of the *ḥakhamim*, all three terms may be synonymous. Elsewhere as well *ḥakhamim* seem synonymous with *sopherim* (cf. Sanh. 11:3) and also with *perushim* (see Rivkin's combined treatment of *Yadayim* 4:6, 7; *T. Yadayim* 2:20; *Yadayim* 4:8; *Yoma* 19b; *T. Ḥagigah* 3:35; *Niddah* 33b; *T. Yoma* 1:8; *Makkot* 1:6; *T.R.H.* 1:15; *Kiddushin* 66a; *ibid.*, 209-220); accordingly, Rivkin, here also, finds grounds for identifying *sopherim* with *perushim* (in essence, two terms both synonymous with a third are therefore synonymous with each other). Cf. Bowker's citations of Rivkin, *op. cit.*, 1, 5, 22. While differing with Rivkin in many respects, Bowker does recognize that *ḥakhamim* are related to the Pharisees described by Josephus (p. 5) and that there are rabbinic passages wherein *ḥakhamim* can be said to be identical with *perushim* (pp. 8f., 12-13, 15); moreover, in certain situations, *ḥakhamim* and *sopherim* can be used identically. Hence, "it follows also that the *sopherim could* be *perushim*, and in places their views are identical.... This is of great importance in considering the Scribes in Mark" (p. 22 n. 3 [italics Bowker's]; cf. 40).

[44] See Moore, I, 43: "The old name, Scribes, was apparently the only one in use in the age from which the Gospels come. In the Tannaite literature scholars are called Hakamim, in the sense of 'the learned,' students are Talmide Hakamim, disciples of the learned, the name Soferim, Scribes, being restricted to the learned of an older time. The sources at our command do not disclose the reason for this change in usage or the date at which the new designation was introduced. It may perhaps be connected with the reorganization of the schools after the destruction of Jerusalem...." Cf. Marcus, *art. cit.*, 155.

[45] See *supra*, end of Chapter Four, and, in this chapter, note 6.

the Passion narrative proper. As it is, he was comfortable transferring one mention of them from Galilee in Chapter 3 to Jerusalem in Judaea in what is now 12:13-17, 34b, but not to any later chapter. Indeed, had he introduced Pharisees into the Passion narrative itself, he would thereby have brought them into contact with chief priests, with scribes, and with elders. The five conspiratorial groups would not then have appeared rigidly compartmentalized into two separate camps; for the pattern would have been broken not only in 2:16 and 7:1, 5 but in the Passion narrative itself. The parameters of Mark's three underlying sources might then have been so camouflaged that we could not even attempt to reconstruct the procedures he followed.

WORKS CONSULTED

BOOKS

Abrahams, I. *Studies in Pharisaism and the Gospels*. Series 1-2, repr. New York, 1967.

Achtemeier, P. J. *Mark*. Philadelphia, 1975.

Albertz, M. *Die synoptischen Streitgespräche*. Berlin, 1921.

Allen, W. C. *The Gospel according to St. Mark*. London, 1915.

Allon, G. *Meḥqarim be-Toledot Yisrael*. Tel Aviv, 1957.

Bacon, B. W. *The Beginnings of Gospel Story*. New Haven, 1909.

——. *The Gospel of Mark: Its Composition and Date*. New Haven, 1925.

——. *Is Mark a Roman Gospel?* Cambridge, Mass., 1919.

Bartlet, J. V. *St. Mark*. Edinburgh, 1922.

Beare, F. W. *The Earliest Records of Jesus*. Nashville, 1962.

Bornkamm, G.; Barth, G.; and Held, H. J. *Tradition and Interpretation in Matthew*. Trans. P. Scott. Philadelphia, 1963.

Bousset, W. *Kyrios Christos*. Trans. J. E. Steely. Nashville, 1970.

Bowker, J. *Jesus and the Pharisees*. Cambridge, 1973.

Brandon, S. G. F. *Jesus and the Zealots*. Manchester, 1967.

Branscomb, B. H. *The Gospel of Mark*. London, 1937.

Büchler, A. *Die Priester und der Cultus im letzten Jahrzehnt des Jerusalemischen Tempels*. Vienna, 1895.

Bultmann, R. *The History of the Synoptic Tradition*. Trans. J. Marsh. Oxford, 1963.

Burkill, T. A. *New Light on the Earliest Gospel: Seven Markan Studies*. Ithaca, 1972.

Cadoux, A. T. *The Sources of the Second Gospel*. New York, 1935.

Catchpole, D. R. *The Trial of Jesus: A Study in the Gospels and Jewish Historiography from 1770 to the Present Day*. Leiden, 1971.

Chwolson, D. *Das letzte Passamahl Christi und der Tag seines Todes*. 2nd edition. Leipzig, 1908.

Conzelmann, H. *A History of Primitive Christianity*. Trans. J. E. Steely. Nashville, 1973.

Dibelius, M. *From Tradition to Gospel*. Trans. B. L. Woolf. New York, 1935.

Donahue, J. R. *Are You the Christ? The Trial Narrative in the Gospel of Mark*. Missoula, Montana, 1973.

Easton, B. S. *The Gospel Before the Gospels*. New York, 1928.

Enslin, M. S. *Christian Beginnings*. Repr. New York, 1956.

Farmer, W. R. *The Synoptic Problem: A Critical Analysis*. New York, 1964.

Fascher, E. *Die formgeschichtliche Methode: eine Darstellung und Kritik*. Giessen, 1924.

Feine, P.; Behm, J.; and Kümmel, W. G. *Introduction to the New Testament*. Trans. A. J. Mattill, Jr. Nashville, 1965.

Finegan, J. *Mark of the Taw*. Richmond, 1972.

Finkel, A. *The Pharisees and the Teacher of Nazareth*. Leiden, 1964.

Finkelstein, L. *The Pharisees*. 2 vols. 3rd edition. Philadelphia, 1962.

Foakes-Jackson, F. J. and Lake, K. *The Beginnings of Christianity*. Vol. I. London, 1920.

Friedländer, G. *The Jewish Sources of the Sermon on the Mount*. Repr. New York, 1969.

Gager, J. G. *Kingdom and Community — The Social World of Early Christianity*. Englewood Cliffs, N.J., 1975.

Geiger, A. *Das Judentum und seine Geschichte*. 2nd edition, Breslau, 1865.
———. *Urschrift und Übersetzungen der Bibel*. Frankfurt a.M., 1928.
Goldstein, M. *Jesus in the Jewish Tradition*. New York, 1950.
Goodman, P. *The Synagogue and the Church*. London, 1908.
Graetz, H. *History of the Jews*. Vol. II. Philadelphia, 1893.
———. *Sinai et Golgotha, ou les origines du judaïsme et du christianisme....* Trans. M. Hess. Paris, 1867.
Grant, F. C. *The Earliest Gospel*. New York, 1943.
———. *The Growth of the Gospels*. New York, 1933.
Graves, R. and Podro, J. *The Nazarene Gospel Restored*. London, 1953.
Güttgemanns, E. *Offene Fragen zur Formgeschichte des Evangeliums*. Munich, 1970.
Hare, D. R. A. *The Theme of Jewish Persecution of Christians in the Gospel According to Matthew*. Cambridge, 1967.
Harnack, A. *The Date of the Acts and of the Synoptic Gospels*. London, 1911.
Herford, R. T. *Christianity in Talmud and Midrash*. London, 1903.
———. *The Pharisees*. New York, 1924.
Jeremias, J. *Jerusalem in the Time of Jesus*. Trans. F. H. and C. H. Cave. Philadelphia, 1969.
Johnson, S. E. *A Commentary on the Gospel according to Mark*. New York, 1960.
Kähler, M. *The So-Called Historical Jesus and the Historic Biblical Christ*. Trans. C. E. Braaten. Philadelphia, 1964.
Kee, H. C. *Community of the New Age: Studies in Mark's Gospel*. Philadelphia, 1977.
———. *Jesus in History*. New York, 1970.
Kelber, W. H. *The Kingdom in Mark: a New Place and a New Time*. Philadelphia, 1974.
Klausner, J. *Jesus of Nazareth*. Trans. H. Danby. Repr. New York, 1943.
Klostermann, E. *Das Markusevangelium*. 2nd edition. Tübingen, 1926.
Knox, J. *Chapters in a Life of Paul*. Nashville, 1950.
Knox, W. L. *The Sources of the Synoptic Gospels: Vol. I — St. Mark*. Cambridge, 1953.
Krenkel, M. *Josephus und Lucas*. Leipzig, 1894.
Kuhn, H. W. *Ältere Sammlungen im Markusevangelium*. Göttingen, 1971.
Lane, W. L. *The Gospel of Mark*. Grand Rapids, 1975.
Lauterbach, J. Z. *Rabbinic Essays*. Cincinnati, 1951.
Lightfoot, R. H. *Locality and Doctrine in the Gospels*. London, 1938.
Lindars, B. *New Testament Apologetic*. London, 1961.
Linnemann, E. *Studien zur Passionsgeschichte*. Göttingen, 1970.
Lohmeyer, E. *Das Evangelium des Markus*. Göttingen, 1937.
———. *Galiläa und Jerusalem*. Göttingen, 1936.
Loisy, A. *The Origins of the New Testament*. Trans. L. P. Jacks. London, 1950.
Manson, T. W. *Studies in the Gospels*. Manchester, 1962.
Mantel, H. *Studies in the History of the Sanhedrin*. Cambridge, Mass. 1961.
Martin, R. P. *Mark: Evangelist and Theologian*. Trowbridge, 1972.
Marxsen, W. *Mark the Evangelist: Studies on the Redaction History of the Gospel*. Trans. J. Boyce *et al*. Nashville, 1969.
Meyer, E. *Ursprung und Anfänge des Christentums*. 3 vols. Berlin, 1921-1923.
Moffatt, J. *An Introduction to the Literature of the New Testament*. New York, 1923.
Montefiore, C. G. *The Synoptic Gospels*. 2 vols. London, 1927.
Montefiore, H. W. *Josephus and the New Testament*. London, 1962. (From *NovT* 4, Fasc. 2 & 4 [1960]).
Moore, G. F. *Judaism*. 3 vols. Cambridge, Mass., 1946.
Neusner, J. *From Politics to Piety: the Emergence of Pharisaic Judaism*. Englewood Cliffs, N.J., 1973.

——. *The Rabbinic Traditions about the Pharisees before 70.* 3 vols. Leiden, 1971.
Olmstead, A. T. *Jesus in the Light of History.* New York, 1942.
Perrin, N. *Rediscovering the Teaching of Jesus.* New York, 1967.
——. *What Is Redaction Criticism?* Philadelphia, 1969.
Pesch, R. *Das Markusevangelium.* Vol. I. Freiburg, 1976.
Pines, Sh. *An Arabic Version of the Testimonium Flavianum and Its Implications.* Jerusalem, 1971.
Quesnell, Q. *The Mind of Mark.* Rome, 1969.
Rawlinson, A. E. J. *St. Mark.* London, 1925.
Riddle, D. W. *Jesus and the Pharisees.* Chicago, 1928.
Robertson, A. T. *The Pharisees and Jesus.* New York, 1920.
Rohde, J. *Rediscovering the Teaching of the Evangelists.* Trans. D. Barton. Philadelphia, 1969.
Sandmel, S. *The Genius of Paul.* New York, 1970.
——. *A Jewish Understanding of the New Testament.* New York, 1960.
Schmidt, K. L. *Der Rahmen der Geschichte Jesu.* Repr. Darmstadt, 1964.
Schram, T. L. *The Use of Ioudaios in the Fourth Gospel.* Utrecht, 1974.
Schürer, E. *Geschichte des jüdischen Volkes im Zeitalter Jesu Christi.* 3rd and 4th editions. 3 vols. Leipzig, 1901-1911; trans. J. Macpherson: *A History of the Jewish People in the Time of Jesus Christ.* 5 vols. Edinburgh, 1885-1890; Vermes-Millar edition: *The History of the Jewish People in the Age of Jesus Christ (175 B.C.-A.D. 135).* Vol. I. Edinburgh, 1973.
Sloyan, G. *Jesus on Trial.* Philadelphia, 1973.
Spivey, R. A. and Smith, D. M., Jr. *Anatomy of the New Testament.* 2nd ed. New York, 1974.
Stein, L. *Die Schrift des Lebens.* 2 vols. Strasbourg, 1872.
Streeter, B. H. *The Four Gospels.* London, 1924.
Sundwall, J. *Die Zusammensetzung des Markusevangeliums.* Abo, 1934.
Swete, H. B. *The Gospel according to St. Mark.* London, 1927.
Taylor, V. *The Formation of the Gospel Tradition.* 2nd ed. Repr. London, 1949.
——. *The Gospel According to St. Mark.* 2nd ed. New York, 1966.
Torrey, C. C. *The Four Gospels: A New Translation.* 2nd ed. New York, 1947.
Tyson, J. *A Study of Early Christianity.* New York, 1973.
Weeden, T. J. *Mark—Traditions in Conflict.* Philadelphia, 1972.
Weiss, J. *Das älteste Evangelium.* Göttingen, 1903.
Wellhausen, J. *Das Evangelium Marci.* 2nd ed. Berlin, 1909.
Wilson, W. R. *The Execution of Jesus.* New York, 1970.
Winter, P. *On the Trial of Jesus.* Berlin, 1961.
Wrede, W. *Das Messiasgeheimnis.* 3rd edition. Göttingen, 1963.
Wright, L. E. *Alterations in the Words of Jesus....* Cambridge, Mass., 1952.
Zeitlin, S. *The Rise and Fall of the Judaean State.* 2 vols. Philadelphia, 1964.

ESSAYS AND ARTICLES

Achtemeier, P. J. "Toward the Isolation of Pre-Markan Miracle Catenae," *JBL* 89 (1970), 265-291.
——. "The Origin and Function of the Pre-Markan Miracle Catenae," *JBL* 91 (1972), 198-221.
Bacon, B. W. "Pharisees and Herodians in Mark," *JBL* 39 (1920), 102-112.
Beare, F. W. "The Sabbath Was Made for Man?" *JBL* 79 (1960), 130-136.
——. Review of *The Synoptic Problem: A Critical Analysis*, by W. R. Farmer. *JBL* 84 (1965), 295-297.
Bennett, W. J., Jr. "The Herodians of Mark's Gospel," *NovT* 17 (1975), 9-14.

Black, M. "Scribe," *IDB*, IV, 246-248.

Boobyer, G. H. "Galilee and Galileans in St. Mark's Gospel," *BJRL* 35 (1952-1953), 334-348.

Brandon, S. G. F. "The Date of the Markan Gospel," *NTS* 7 (1960-1961), 126-141.

Brown, R. Review of *The Passion in Mark: Studies on Mark 14-16*, ed. W. H. Kelber. *CBQ* 39 (1977), 283-285.

Budesheim, T. L. "Jesus and the Disciples in Conflict with Judaism," *ZNW* 62 (1971), 190-209.

Burkill, T. A. "Anti-Semitism in St. Mark's Gospel," *NovT* 3 (1959), 34-53; also in French, "L'antisémitisme dans l'évangile selon Saint Marc," *RHR* 154 (1958), 10-31.

———. "St. Mark's Philosophy of the Passion," *NovT* 2 (1958), 245-271.

———. "Sanhedrin," *IDB*, IV, 214-218.

———. "Strain on the Secret: an Examination of Mark 11:1-13:37," *ZNW* 51 (1960), 31-46.

Cheyne, T. K. "Herodians," *EB*, II, Col. 2043.

Cook, M. J. "Jesus and the Pharisees: the Problem as It Stands Today," *JES* 15 (Summer 1978; tentative).

———. "Judaism, Early Rabbinic," *IDB* Suppl. Vol., 499-505.

———. "Judaism, Hellenistic," *IDB* Suppl. Vol., 505-509.

Danby, H. "The Bearing of the Rabbinical Criminal Code on the Jewish Trial Narratives in the Gospels," *JTS* 21 (1919), 51-76.

Dodd, C. H. "The Framework of the Gospel Narrative," in *In Search of the Historical Jesus*, H. K. McArthur, ed. New York, 1969, 109-118.

Donahue, J. R. "Introduction: From Passion Traditions to Passion Narrative," in *The Passion in Mark: Studies on Mark 14-16*, W. H. Kelber, ed. Philadelphia, 1976, 1-20.

———. "Temple, Trial, and Royal Christology (Mark 14:53-65)," in *ibid.*, 61-79.

Easton, B. S. "A Primitive Tradition in Mark," in *Studies in Early Christianity*, S. J. Case, ed. New York, 1928, 83-101.

Enslin, M. S. "Once Again, Luke and Paul," *ZNW* 61 (1970), 253-271.

———. "Paul and Gamaliel," *JR* 7 (1927), 360-375.

Farrer, A. M. "On Dispensing with Q," in *Studies in the Gospels: Essays in Memory of R. H. Lightfoot*, D. E. Nineham, ed. Oxford, 1955, 55-86.

Gilmour, S. M. "The Gospel According to St. Luke: Introduction and Exegesis," *IB*, VIII.

Grant, F. C. "The Gospel According to St. Mark: Introduction and Exegesis," *IB*, VII.

———. Review of *The Synoptic Problem: A Critical Analysis*, by W. R. Farmer. *Interp* 19 (1965), 352-354.

Guttmann, A. "The End of the Jewish Sacrificial Cult," *HUCA* 38 (1967), 137-148.

Hamilton, N. Q. "Resurrection Tradition and the Composition of Mark," *JBL* 84 (1965), 415-421.

Hay, L. S. "The Son of Man in Mark 2.10 and 2.28," *JBL* 89 (1970), 69-75.

Hultgren, A. J. "The Formation of the Sabbath Pericope in Mark 2:23-28," *JBL* 91 (1972), 38-43.

Karnetski, M. "Die galiläische Redaktion im Markusevangelium," *ZNW* 52 (1961), 228-272.

Kelber, W. H. "Conclusion: From Passion Narrative to Gospel," in *The Passion in Mark: Studies on Mark 14-16*, W. H. Kelber, ed. Philadelphia, 1976, 153-180.

———. Review of *Ältere Sammlungen im Markusevangelium*, by H. W. Kuhn, *JBL* 93 (1974), 306-308.

Klijn, A. F. J. "Scribes, Pharisees, Highpriests and Elders in the New Testament," *NovT* 3 (1959), 259-267.

Kohler, K. "Pharisees," *JE*, IX, 661-666.

Loewe, H. "Pharisaism," in *Judaism and Christianity*, W. O. E. Oesterley, H. Loewe and E. I. J. Rosenthal, eds. Repr. New York, 1969, 103-190.

Manson, T. W. "The Life of Jesus," *BJRL* 28 (1944), 119-136.

——. "Studies in the Gospels and Epistles," in *In Search of the Historical Jesus*, H. K. McArthur, ed. New York, 1969, 23-32.

Marcus, R. A. "The Pharisees in the Light of Modern Scholarship," *JR* 32 (1952), 153-164.

Mattill, A. J., Jr. "The Jesus-Paul Parallels and the Purpose of Luke-Acts: H. H. Evans Reconsidered," *NovT* 17 (1975), 15-46.

Moore, G. F. "Christian Writers on Judaism," *HTR* 14 (1921), 197-254.

——. "The Rise of Normative Judaism," *HTR* 17 (1924), 307-373.

Niederwimmer, K. "Johannes Markus und die Frage nach dem Verfasser des zweiten Evangeliums," *ZNW* 58 (1967), 172-188.

Petrie, S. " 'Q' Is Only What You Make It," *NovT* 3 (1959), 28-33.

Purdy, A. C. "Paul the Apostle," *IDB*, III, 681-704.

Reedy, C. J. "Mk. 8:31-11:10 and the Gospel Ending: A Redaction Study," *CBQ* 34 (1972), 188-197.

Rivkin, E. "Beth Din, Boulé, Sanhedrin: A Tragedy of Errors," *HUCA* 46 (1975), 181-199.

——. "Defining the Pharisees: the Tannaitic Sources," *HUCA* 40-41 (1969-1970), 205-249.

——. "Prolegomenon" to *Judaism and Christianity*, W. O. E. Oesterley, H. Loewe and E. I. J. Rosenthal, eds. Repr. New York, 1969, vii-lxx.

Rowley, H. H. "The Herodians in the Gospels," *JTS* 41 (1940), 14-27.

Sandmel, S. "Herodians," *IDB*, II, 594-595.

——. "The Trial of Jesus: Reservations," *Judaism* 20 (1971), 69-74.

Schreiber, J. "Die Christologie des Markus," *ZTK* 58 (1961), 154-183.

Scroggs, R. "The Earliest Christian Communities as Sectarian Movement," *Christianity, Judaism and Other Greco-Roman Cults: Studies for Morton Smith at Sixty*, J. Neusner, ed. Part Two. Leiden, 1975, 1-23.

Smith, M. "Palestinian Judaism in the First Century," in *Israel: Its Role in Civilization*, Moshe Davis, ed. New York, 1956.

Stein, R. H. "The 'Redaktionsgeschichtlich' Investigation of a Markan Seam (Mc 1:21f.)," *ZNW* 61 (1970), 70-94.

——. "What is Redaktionsgeschichte?" *JBL* 88 (1969), 45-56.

Strecker, G. "Die Leidens- und Auferstehungsvoraussagen im Markusevangelium," *ZTK* 64 (1967), 16-39.

Talbert, C. H. and McKnight, E. V. "Can the Griesbach Hypothesis Be Falsified?" *JBL* 91 (1972), 338-368.

Torrey, C. C. "The Date of Mark," *Documents of the Primitive Church*, New York, 1941, 1-40.

Weber, J. C., Jr. "Jesus' Opponents in the Gospel of Mark," *JBibRelig* 34 (1966): 214-222.

Winter, P. "Excursus II — Josephus on Jesus and James: *Ant.* xviii 3, 3 (63-4) and xx 9, 1 (200-3)," in *The History of the Jewish People in the Age of Jesus Christ (175 B.C.-A.D. 135)*, by E. Schürer. Vermes-Millar edition. Vol. I. Edinburgh, 1973, 428-441.

INDEX OF AUTHORS

Abrahams, I. 80
Achtemeier, P. J. 12, 36, 54ff., 77, 79, 95
Albertz, M. 31ff., 34ff., 44, 45, 46f., 48ff., 61, 80ff.
Allen, W. C. 12
Allon, G. 85f.
Bacon, B. W. 6, 10ff., 17, 19, 29, 33, 34, 41, 45, 46, 48, 64, 65, 70, 72, 74
Barth, G. 8
Bartlet, J. V. 12
Beare, F. W. 2, 44
Behm, J. 6, 12
Bennett, W. J., Jr. 17
Black, M. 95f.
Boobyer, G. H. 14
Bornkamm, G. 8f.
Bousset, W. 33, 45
Bowker, J. 70, 72, 96f.
Brandon, S. G. F. 6, 12, 17, 56f.
Branscomb, B. H. 6, 17, 33, 34, 35ff., 40f., 45, 63ff., 64, 72, 85
Brown, R. 55f.
Büchler, A. 72, 92
Budesheim, T. L. 35
Bultmann, R. 30, 32f., 33f., 35f., 44, 45, 46, 48, 52, 53ff., 61, 64f., 65f., 66, 70ff., 80
Burkill, T. A. 2, 6, 20f., 29, 32, 35, 40, 52, 54, 61, 66, 70, 74, 95
Cadoux, A. T. 19, 41
Catchpole, D. R. 16, 80
Cheyne, T. K. 17
Chwolson, D. 72, 92
Conzelmann, H. 13
Cook, M. J. 59, 73, 84, 85
Danby, H. 16, 95
Dibelius, M. 8ff., 29, 30, 32, 35, 44, 46, 48, 52, 53ff., 61, 64ff., 67
Dodd, C. H. 35
Donahue, J. R. 6, 7f., 8, 9, 30ff., 35, 45, 48, 52, 54ff., 61, 77, 95
Easton, B. S. 32, 35f., 36, 40ff., 46, 61, 80
Enslin, M. S. 3ff., 6, 13, 20
Farmer, W. R. 2
Farrer, A. M. 3
Fascher, E. 33f., 34f., 35, 45, 80

Feine, P. 6, 12
Finegan, J. 12
Finkel, A. 18, 80
Finkelstein, L. 72, 85
Foakes-Jackson, F. J. 17, 20
Friedländer, G. 80
Geiger, A. 80, 85
Gilmour, S. M. 20
Goldstein, M. 16
Goodman, P. 80
Graetz, H. 80
Grant, F. C. 2, 14, 16, 20, 34, 36ff., 45, 49, 52, 61f., 70f., 80
Graves, R. 80
Güttgemanns, E. 54
Guttmann, A. 17
Hamilton, N. Q. 13
Hare, D. R. A. 74f.
Harnack, A. 6
Hay, L. S. 44
Held, H. J. 8
Herford, R. T. 16, 80, 85
Hultgren, A. J. 35, 44f.
Jeremias, J. 17, 18f., 23f., 72, 85
Johnson, S. E. 12
Kähler, M. 52
Karnetski, M. 13, 14
Kee, H. C. 9, 12f., 13, 25, 31f., 35, 45, 46, 54
Kelber, W. H. 13, 30, 36f., 52, 54f.
Klausner, J. 16, 19, 72, 80, 91f.
Klijn, A. F. J. 25, 27f.
Klostermann, E. 25, 33, 34, 45, 61, 72
Knox, J. 13
Knox, W. L. 20f., 30, 32, 34, 35, 40f., 41, 64, 66f., 80
Kohler, K. 80
Krenkel, M. 20
Kuhn, H. W. 36f.
Kümmel, W. G. 6, 12
Lake, K. 17, 20
Lane, W. L. 12
Lauterbach, J. Z. 16, 80, 85
Lightfoot, R. H. 13
Lindars, B. 49
Linnemann, E. 54
Loewe, H. 59, 84
Lohmeyer, E. 13, 45, 49

Loisy, A. 49f., 80
Manson, T. W. 12, 35, 40, 45, 46f.
Mantel, H. 59f., 80, 95
Marcus, R. A. 72, 80, 96
Martin, R. P. 6, 8, 12
Marxsen, W. 8f., 13, 52
Mattill, A. J., Jr. 88
McKnight, E. V. 2
Meyer, E. 72
Moffatt, J. 6f., 20, 49, 63
Montefiore, C. G. 45
Montefiore, H. W. 20
Moore, G. F. 72, 80, 84, 96ff.
Neusner, J. 81, 85f., 92
Niederwimmer, K. 12
Olmstead, A. T. 18, 45, 72, 92
Perrin, N. 2, 8, 45
Pesch, R. 12
Petrie, S. 3
Pines, Sh. 15
Podro, J. 80
Purdy, A. C. 13
Quesnell, Q. 49
Rawlinson, A. E. J. 34, 44, 45f.
Reedy, C. J. 49, 61
Riddle, D. W. 3ff., 12, 18ff., 56ff., 65, 70, 74, 80
Rivkin, E. 59f., 72, 75, 84, 85f., 95ff.
Robertson, A. T. 18
Rohde, J. 8
Rowley, H. H. 17

Sandmel, S. 13, 16, 41, 59, 80, 84
Schmidt, K. L. 34, 35, 44, 61
Schram, T. L. 4
Schreiber, J. 14
Schürer, E. 15, 17, 72
Scroggs, R. 93
Sloyan, G. 24, 52, 53ff., 94
Smith, D. M., Jr. 6, 7f., 8f.
Smith, M. 92, 93
Spivey, R. A. 6, 7f., 8f.
Stein, L. 80
Stein, R. H. 8, 34f., 35
Strecker, G. 61
Streeter, B. H. 6
Sundwall, J. 35
Swete, H. B. 12, 14
Talbert, C. H. 2
Taylor, V. 12, 17, 23, 26, 29, 34f., 35, 36f., 40ff., 44, 45f., 46, 47ff., 48, 49, 52, 54, 55f., 61, 64, 65ff., 70, 72, 80
Torrey, C. C. 6, 45
Tyson, J. 2, 12
Weeden, T. J. 13, 45, 64, 65f.
Weiss, J. 41
Wellhausen, J. 45, 70
Wilson, W. R. 52
Winter, P. 15, 17, 48, 50, 52, 53, 54, 68ff.
Wrede, W. 49
Wright, L. E. 80
Zeitlin, S. 85, 95